Year Round

DAIRY COOKBOOK

Executive Editor	Nick Rowe
Managing Editor	Emily Anderson
Editor	Emma Callery
Designer	Karen Raison
Proofreader	Kate Parker
Index	Hilary Bird
Photographer	Steve Lee
Props Stylist	Jo Harris
Food Stylists	Joss Herd
	Sara Lewis
Recipes created by	Pat Alburey
	Kathryn Hawkins
	Sue McMahon
	Kate Moseley
Calorie Analysis	Dr Wendy Doyle
Recipe Testers	Iain Anderson
	Penny Arnold
	Jan Bailey
	Helen Cookson
	Carolyn Glazebrook
	Lucy Goodman
	Kristen Helsby
	Natalie Meadowcroft
	Sandra Meadowcroft
	Anne-Marie Neild
	Emma Selby
	Pam Shore
	Jane Smallwood
	Marjorie Wood
Production	Teresa Wellborne

Eaglemoss Consumer Publications Ltd
Electra House, Electra Way,
Crewe, Cheshire, CW1 6WZ
Telephone 01270 270050
Website www.dairydiary.co.uk

First printed March 2005

© Eaglemoss Consumer Publications Ltd

Contents

Spring heralds new life, and what better way to celebrate it than with foods such as lamb, asparagus and traditional pancakes. There's no better time to enjoy good food than a feast at Easter.

Enjoy our British summer at home: let your tastebuds do the travelling for you with delicious meals from Greece, Spain and Mexico, plus, of course, many favourite recipes such as salmon with cucumber sauce.

After the harvest comes the feast, and this one includes warming soups, spicy salads, interesting savoury fair using British cheeses, and some wonderful dishes for the season's ripening apples, plums and pears.

This is the season for comfort food. Try the smooth, creamy soups, a wonderfully filling lasagne, flavoursome stews and a great savoury crumble. Then indulge yourself with a rich dessert made from winter fruits or luxurious chocolate.

Introduction

The *Year Round Dairy Cookbook* has more than 130 seasonal recipes to give your tastebuds a treat throughout the whole year.

For centuries, people ate what was available, so our diet changed as the year passed. Now, in the age of global travel and supermarkets, we can eat what we feel like all year round.

But there are many reasons to eat what is in season. Our food is more likely to be fresh, and grown without being forced to ripen early or late. The ingredients have not travelled thousands of miles to reach our plate – instead, what we are eating is more likely to be local produce, so we are sustaining businesses in our own area. Eating seasonally also keeps us in step with the natural rhythm of the year.

This book has a section on each season, subdivided into recipes for snacks, main courses and desserts. Many of the recipes are modern versions of traditional British dishes (often with a contemporary twist), but there are recipes from around the world too. Each recipe has been tested by the writer, by an ordinary cook and a stylist to ensure success.

With each recipe, you'll find preparation and cooking times, calorie counts and details of fat content, together with cook's tips to make the job easier, or to suggest variations. Conversion charts for dry weights, liquids and oven temperatures are given overleaf.

Spring

Vegetables: asparagus, baby carrots, cauliflowers, morel mushrooms, new potatoes, purple sprouting broccoli, radishes, sea kale, sorrel, spinach, spring cabbages, spring greens, spring onions, wild garlic
Fruit: gooseberries, kumquats, rhubarb
Meat: lamb
Fish: crab, dab, Dover sole, flounders, halibut, monkfish, plaice, scallops, wild salmon
Other: herbs (chives, mint, rosemary, sage, thyme)

Summer

Vegetables: artichokes, aubergines, beetroot, broad beans, broccoli, cauliflower, courgettes, cucumbers, fennel, Jersey Royal new potatoes, onions, peas, radishes, runner beans, salad leaves, sweet peppers
Fruit: apricots, blackcurrants, blueberries, cherries, gooseberries, greengages, nectarines, peaches, raspberries, redcurrants, strawberries, tomatoes
Meat: beef, chicken, pork
Fish: herrings, sardines, sea bream, sea trout, wild salmon
Other: herbs (basil, coriander, oregano)

Autumn

Vegetables: aubergines, beetroot, Brussel sprouts, butternut squash, carrots, cauliflower, celeriac, courgettes, curly kale, parsnips, pumpkins, rhubarb (forced), swedes, sweetcorn, Swiss chard, turnips, wild mushrooms

Fruit: apples (Cox's Orange Pippin, Egremont Russet, Bramley's Seedling), blackberries, figs, greengages, pears (Comice, Conference), plums, quince, raspberries, tomatoes

Meat: partridge, rabbit, wild duck, woodcock, wood pigeons

Fish: brill, Dover sole, mussels, skate, tuna

Other: blue cheese, walnuts

Winter

Vegetables: Brussel sprouts, cabbages, carrots, celeriac, chicory, curly kale, Jerusalem artichokes, kohlrabi, leeks, parsnips, potatoes, purple sprouting broccoli, salsify, Savoy cabbage, spinach

Fruit: apples (Bramley), clementines, cranberries, grapefruit, kumquats, lychees, pineapples, quince, satsumas, Seville oranges, tangerines

Meat: duck, Parma ham, partridge, pheasant

Fish: bream, salmon, scallops, turbot

Other: almonds, chestnuts, dates, figs, hazelnuts, walnuts, Stilton cheese

Information for cooks

Metric and imperial measurements are given in all the recipes. Follow one or the other set and do not mix the two as they are not interchangeable. Unless otherwise specified, always use medium-sized eggs, fruit and vegetables, and fresh herbs.

Dry weight conversions

Recommended grams (g)	Imperial ounces (oz)
15	½
25	1
50	2
75	3
110	4 (¼lb)
150	5
175	6
200	7
225	8 (½lb)
250	9
275	10
300	11
350	12 (¾lb)
375	13
400	14
425	15
450	16 (1lb)
500	1lb 2oz
680	1½lb
750	1lb 10oz
900	2lb

These quantities are not exact, but they have been calculated to give proportionately correct measurements.

Spoon measures

1 tablespoon	= 3 level teaspoons
1 level tablespoon	= 15ml
1 level teaspoon	= 5ml

If greater accuracy is not required:

1 rounded teaspoon	= 2 level teaspoons
1 heaped teaspoon	= 3 level teaspoons or 1 level tablespoon

Liquid conversions

Metric (ml)	Imperial (fl oz)	Cups
15	½	1 tbsp (level)
30	1	⅛
60	2	¼
90	3	⅜
125	4	½
150	5 (¼ pint)	⅔
175	6	¾
225	8	1
300	10 (½ pint)	1¼
350	12	1½
450	16	2
500	18	2¼
600	20 (1 pint)	2½
900	1½ pints	3¾
1 litre	1¾ pints	1 quart (4 cups)
1.25 litres	2 pints	1¼ quarts
1.5 litres	2½ pints	3 US pints
2 litres	3½ pints	2 quarts

568ml = 1 UK pint	(20fl oz)	16fl oz = 1 US pint

These quantities are not exact, but they have been calculated to give proportionately correct measurements.

Estimated average requirements

Estimated average requirements (EARs) are the amount of nutrients or energy required each day for the average adult.

	Calories	Saturated fat	Salt	Fibre
Women	1900	11g	less than 6g	18g
Men	2550	11g	less than 6g	18g

Oven temperatures

°C	°F	Gas mark	Description
110	225	¼	cool
120/130	250	½	cool
140	275	1	very low
150	300	2	very low
160/170	325	3	low to moderate
180	350	4	moderate
190	375	5	moderately hot
200	400	6	hot
220	425	7	hot
230	450	8	hot
240	475	9	very hot

Guide to recommended equivalent settings, not exact conversions. Always refer to your cooker instruction book.

Grilling times: fish

Type of fish	Grilling time
Cod (steak)	5–6 min each side
Dover sole (whole)	4–6 min each side
Dover sole (fillet)	2–3 min each side
Halibut (steak)	5–6 min each side
Herring (whole)	4–5 min each side
Mackerel (whole)	6–7 min each side
Monkfish (steak)	5–6 min each side
Plaice (whole)	4–6 min each side
Plaice (fillet)	2–3 min each side
Salmon (steak)	5–6 min each side
Tuna (steak)	1–2 min each side

Times given for fish weighing approximately 175–225g (6–8 oz).

Roasting times: meat

Set oven temperature to 180°C/350°F/Gas 4.

	Cooking time per 450g/1lb	Extra cooking time
Beef		
Rare	20 min	20 min
Medium	25 min	25 min
Well done	30 min	30 min
Lamb		
Medium	25 min	25 min
Well done	30 min	30 min
Pork		
Medium	30 min	30 min
Well done	35 min	35 min

Let the cooked meat rest for 5–15 minutes before carving to allow the juices to be reabsorbed and to make carving easier.

Steaming times: vegetables

Vegetable	Steaming time
Asparagus	5–7 min
Beansprouts	3–4 min
Beetroot (sliced)	5–7 min
Broccoli (florets)	5–7 min
Brussel sprouts	5–7 min
Cabbage (chopped)	4–6 min
Cauliflower (florets)	5–7 min
Carrots (thickly sliced)	5–7 min
Courgettes (sliced)	3–5 min
Green beans	5–7 min
Leeks	5–8 min
Mangetout peas	3–5 min
Peas	3–5 min
Potatoes (cubed)	5–7 min

Times given are for steaming from when water has started to boil.

Roasting times: poultry

	Oven temperature	Cooking time per 450g/1lb	Extra cooking time	Resting time
Chicken	200°C/400°F/Gas 6	20 min	30 min	15 min
Turkey (stuffed weight)				
small (under 6kg/13lb)	200°C/400°F/Gas 6	12 min	20 min	30 min
large	180°C/350°F/Gas 4	16 min	—	30 min
Duck	200°C/400°F/Gas 6 for 45 min then 180°C/350°F/Gas 4	35 min	—	15 min

spring

French onion soup

A classic, yet healthy, comfort food, this soup is perfect to warm you up after an invigorating spring stroll.

10 minutes preparation time
50 minutes cooking time
211 Kcal per portion
13.2g fat per portion of which
8.1g is saturated
4 servings
Suitable for freezing

Butter 40g (1½oz)

Onions 3, peeled and cut into fine rings

Beef stock 900ml (1½ pints)

Dry sherry 2 tsp (optional)

Salt and freshly ground black pepper

French bread 4 slices, 2.5cm (1in) thick

Cheddar cheese 50g (2oz), grated

1 In a large saucepan, melt the butter and fry the onions gently, until soft. This will take 10–15 minutes.

2 Pour the stock into the saucepan, and bring to the boil. Simmer for 35–40 minutes.

3 Add the sherry, if using, and season to taste. Pour into a flameproof dish or individual dishes and float the bread on top. Sprinkle with cheese and brown under a hot grill.

Cook's tips
•**Cooking the onions really slowly adds a sweetness to the soup. Do not let the onions or butter burn or you will get a bitter taste.**
•**Go easy on the seasoning, especially if using a ready-made stock as they can be very salty.**

Quick minestrone

This is a great recipe for serving an impromptu gathering as you can make as big a pot of soup as you need and add whatever is in the vegetable rack.

15 minutes preparation time
30 minutes cooking time
195 Kcal per portion
8.5g fat per portion of which
2g is saturated
4 servings
Suitable for vegetarians

Oil 2 tbsp

Onion 1, peeled and chopped

Garlic 1 fat clove, peeled and chopped

Carrot 1, peeled and diced

Celery 2 sticks, chopped

Potato 1, peeled and diced

Courgette 1 medium to large, trimmed and diced

Green beans 100g (3½oz), trimmed and cut into short lengths

Vegetable stock 1–1.25 litres (1¾–2 pints)

Mini pasta (conchigliette or similar) 50g (2oz)

Frozen peas 50g (2oz)

Tomatoes 2, deseeded and diced

Salt and freshly ground black pepper

Chopped parsley a good handful

Parmesan cheese freshly grated, 2 tsp per person

1 Heat the oil in a large, deep, lidded saucepan. Add the onion, garlic, carrot and celery and fry gently for 5 minutes.

2 Add the potato, courgette and beans and cook for another 5 minutes with the lid on the saucepan.

3 Pour in 1 litre (1¾ pints) of stock. Bring to the boil for 5 minutes and then add the pasta, part cover and cook for 10 minutes, adding more stock if you like. Tip in the peas and then, after another couple of minutes, add the tomato dice and leave the soup for a further minute.

4 Season well. Spoon into bowls and sprinkle with lots of parsley and freshly grated Parmesan.

Roast new potato & bean salad

Enjoy the fine flavour of Jersey Royals, which are available from May onwards, in this colourful salad. The contrasting textures work perfectly together.

20 minutes preparation time
40 minutes cooking time
225 Kcal per portion
12.1g fat per portion of which
1.6g is saturated
4 servings
Suitable for vegetarians

Small new potatoes 500g (1lb 2oz), washed

Garlic 1 fat clove, unpeeled

Olive oil 4 tbsp

Runner beans 110g (4oz), trimmed and cut diagonally

French or green beans 110g (4oz), trimmed and cut into three

Shelled broad beans 110g (4oz)

Salt and freshly ground black pepper

Cider vinegar 1 tbsp

Cherry tomatoes 10–12, halved

Capers 1 tbsp

Chopped chives a handful

1 Preheat the oven to 200°C/400°F/ Gas 6. Put the potatoes and garlic in a roasting tin. Drizzle with 1 tbsp of oil and use your hands to coat the potatoes with oil. Roast in the oven for 35–40 minutes, shaking the tin occasionally, until the potatoes are browned and softened.

2 Meanwhile, bring a large saucepan of salted water to the boil and add the runner beans, French or green beans and broad beans. Bring back to the boil and cook for 3–4 minutes until just tender. Drain, refresh under cold running water, then drain again.

3 When the potatoes and garlic are cooked, remove from the oven. Squeeze the garlic purée from its skin into a small bowl and mash with salt and pepper. Blend in the vinegar and the remaining oil.

4 Tip the beans, tomatoes and capers into a large bowl and carefully toss them in the dressing. Add the warm potatoes and mix carefully again. Sprinkle with chives and more seasoning. Serve warm.

Broad beans freshly podded are perfect when lightly steamed and served with melted butter and a slice of crusty brown bread. When combined with other beans they are even better.

Cook's tips
•Cook green vegetables in as little water as possible and for the shortest time, to preserve the vitamins.
•To save time, just boil the potatoes for about 25 minutes rather than roasting them. Alternatively, speed up the roasting by parboiling the potatoes for 10 minutes and then roasting for a further 20 minutes.

Bubble & squeakers

Traditional British fair with a contemporary twist using vine tomatoes and balsamic vinegar.

20 minutes preparation time
35 minutes cooking time
325 Kcal per portion
17.1g fat per portion of which
6.1g is saturated
4 servings
Suitable for vegetarians

Potatoes 680g (1½lb), peeled and cut into chunks

Spring greens 225g (8oz), washed well

Milk 6 tbsp

Butter a generous knob

Cheddar cheese 50g (2oz), grated

Salt and freshly ground black pepper

Olive oil 3 tbsp

Cherry tomatoes 16, on the vine (or 4 plum tomatoes, halved)

Thyme sprigs a handful, lightly crushed

Balsamic vinegar 2 tbsp

1 Put the potatoes into a lidded saucepan with enough lightly salted boiling water to just cover them. Cover and cook for 12–14 minutes until tender. Cut out the thick central vein in the leaves of the spring greens and chop the leaves roughly into shortish, finger-width shreds.

2 Drain the potatoes over another saucepan to reserve the liquid for cooking the greens. Bring this to the boil, add the greens to the saucepan and cook, uncovered, for 3 minutes until just tender.

3 Meanwhile, tip the potatoes back into their saucepan and dry over a low heat for half a minute. Add the milk and butter, bring to the boil, take off the heat, and mash until smooth. Beat in the cheese. Drain the greens thoroughly and stir them into the mash and season well.

4 Heat a large frying pan, add 1 tbsp of oil, the tomatoes (in pairs on the stem) and the thyme. Cook over a medium heat for about 5 minutes, turning them a couple of times, until softened. Remove from the pan and set aside in a warm oven. Discard the thyme sprigs.

5 While the tomatoes cook, divide the potato mixture into eight. Form into balls and flatten to rounds about 7.5cm (3in) across. Cook in the frying pan, using the rest of the oil, over a medium to low heat for 4 minutes. Turn them over and cook for another 3 minutes until crispy and browned on both sides. If the pan isn't big enough, cook in two batches, keeping the cooked cakes warm in the oven.

6 Place Bubble and Squeakers onto hot plates, arrange pairs of tomatoes next to each one and drizzle with balsamic vinegar.

Cook's tips

• Choose floury potatoes for this old favourite; King Edwards, Maris Piper or Estima.
• Make the cakes earlier in the day, or the day before. Keep them covered in the fridge and cook for a couple of minutes longer to heat properly.
• Use cabbage or leeks if you can't get spring greens, but the greens have a more robust flavour.

Courgette & trout roulade

This impressive, yet simple, roulade is ideal for a light lunch. The subtle taste of the herbs really do complement the flavour of the fish.

15 minutes preparation time
25 minutes cooking time plus chilling
292 Kcal per portion
24.3g fat per portion of which
13.7g is saturated
8 servings

Butter 50g (2oz)

Courgettes 2, totalling about 225g (8oz), coarsely grated

Plain flour 3 tbsp

Milk 300ml (½ pint)

Eggs 4, separated

Spring onions 4, trimmed and chopped

Salt and freshly ground black pepper

Chopped parsley a generous handful

Mascarpone cheese 250g tub

Tartare sauce 1–2 tbsp

Smoked trout 125g pack, flaked

Chopped chives about 1 tbsp

Dill sprigs about 6, torn into smaller pieces

1 Preheat the oven to 200°C/400°F/ Gas 6. Line a Swiss roll tin measuring 33 x 23cm (13 x 9in) with greased baking parchment. Melt half the butter in a frying pan, add the courgettes and cook over a medium heat for 3–4 minutes until softened but not brown. Take off the heat.

2 Meanwhile, melt the rest of the butter in a saucepan, add the flour and beat well to a thick paste. Add the milk gradually, beating well to make a smooth sauce and simmer for 2–3 minutes. Take off the heat and cool for a couple of minutes. Beat in the egg yolks and then the cooked courgettes, spring onions, plenty of seasoning and the parsley.

3 Whisk the egg whites until just firm. Mix a spoonful into the courgette sauce and then fold in the rest. Spoon the mixture into the tin, spreading it into the corners.

4 Bake in the middle of the oven for 15–18 minutes until risen and just set. Put a piece of baking parchmnet on a folded clean tea towel on the work surface and turn the roulade out onto the paper. Remove the lining paper and cool for about 30 minutes.

5 Soften the cheese in the tub, add the tartare sauce and spread the mixture over the roulade, leaving a thin border round the edges. Scatter flakes of fish over the top and then sprinkle with the herbs. Season.

6 Roll up the roulade from one of the short edges, using the paper to help. Roll it quite tightly then lift it and place it, join down, onto a plate.

7 Chill, but bring back to room temperature for about 10 minutes before slicing and serving.

Cook's tips
• **The roulade will keep in the fridge, covered, for 3–4 days.**
• **Add horseradish sauce instead of tartare sauce.**

Spicy lamb burgers

Home-made burgers are easy to make, and taste much better than the pre-packed variety. Buy good-quality minced lamb, which is at its best in spring.

10 minutes preparation time plus chilling
6 minutes cooking time
309 Kcal per portion
22.6g fat per portion of which
9.1g is saturated
4 servings
Suitable for freezing

Shallot or small onion 1, peeled and finely chopped

Garlic 1 clove, peeled and finely chopped

Root ginger 1 tbsp, coarsely grated

Chopped coriander 4 tbsp

Ground cumin ½ tsp

Ground coriander ½ tsp

Ground cinnamon ½ tsp

Mild chilli powder ½ tsp

Ground cardamom a good pinch

Minced lamb 500g (1lb 2oz)

Grape seed or sunflower oil 2 tbsp

Salt and freshly ground black pepper

1 Mix the shallot or onion, garlic, ginger, herbs and spices in a large bowl. Add the lamb and scrunch it all together with your hands until it's evenly mixed.

2 Divide the mixture into eight and lightly shape each portion into a round and flatten with your hand to make burgers about 8cm (3¼in) in diameter. Cover and chill for 30 minutes if you have time.

3 Heat a large frying pan, lightly oil the burgers and season with salt and pepper. Cook the burgers for 2–3 minutes over a medium heat, pressing them down lightly in the pan with a spatula. Turn them over and cook for another 2–3 minutes or 5 minutes if you prefer more well done burgers.

4 Serve the burgers on slices of bread with onion slices, lots of salad and a sweet chilli sauce.

If you are not too keen on spicy food, use parsley instead of coriander and just add cinnamon, leaving out the other spices. Sliced red onion sprinkled on top adds that finishing touch.

Cook's tip

•**If you can, make the burgers the day before you intend to cook them because then the spices have more time to blend into the meat. Double wrap them in cling film to prevent the garlic and spice infiltrating the more sensitive dairy items in your fridge!**

Chicken & Stilton salad

A clever variation on Caesar salad that celebrates the flavour of Stilton, one of the best British cheeses. Very easy to make, and very moreish!

10 minutes preparation time
25 minutes cooking time
654 Kcal per portion
49.4g fat per portion of which
18g is saturated
4 servings

Chicken 4 thighs, skin on but excess skin and fat trimmed

Garlic 1 clove, peeled and left whole

Olive oil 1–2 tbsp

Bread 2 thick slices white, crusts removed, cut into small cubes

Little Gem lettuces 3

Stilton cheese 75g (3oz)

For the dressing:
Lemon juice 1 tbsp

Mayonnaise 1 tbsp

Soured cream 142ml pot

Anchovies 50g can, drained, rinsed if preferred, chopped

1 Heat a non-strick frying pan, add the chicken thighs, flattened out a little, skin side down, and cook for 10 minutes with the garlic clove in the pan. Turn the thighs over and cook for another 10 minutes, adding a little oil if necessary, until cooked through. Remove the chicken from the pan and leave to cool for about 10 minutes.

2 Add the oil to the chicken juices and garlic in the pan and, when hot, add the bread cubes and cook for a couple of minutes, stirring occasionally, until they turn crisp and golden. Set aside. Discard the garlic.

3 Pull the lettuce leaves apart and divide them, whole or torn, between four shallow bowls or plates.

4 Remove the skin and bones from the chicken and cut or tear the meat into chunky strips. Arrange these on the leaves.

5 Make the dressing by whisking the lemon juice, mayonnaise and soured cream in a small bowl. Gently stir in the anchovies and then spoon the dressing over each salad. Scatter crumbled Stilton and the croûtons over the top.

Cook's tips

•**For extra speed, use ready-cooked chicken portions or chicken left over from a roast dinner.**
•**Wash the lettuce well and put in a polybag in the fridge to crisp up for a crunchy salad.**
•**Try Roquefort or Dolcelatte cheese and Cos lettuce.**

Soda bread pizzas

Perfect for a drizzly Saturday at home. Enjoy creating these simple pizzas with your children and, when the pizzas are cooked, enjoy eating them too!

25 minutes preparation time
20 minutes cooking time
406 Kcal per portion
14.2g fat per portion of which
4.6g is saturated
4 servings

For the topping:

Olive oil 2 tsp

Onion 1 small, peeled and diced

Garlic 1 clove, peeled and crushed

Chopped tomatoes 200g can

Salt and freshly ground black pepper

Sugar a good pinch

Double Gloucester cheese 75g (3oz), grated

Kabanos sausages 2, totalling 75g (3oz), sliced

Cup mushrooms 75g (3oz), wiped and sliced

Basil 8 leaves, finely shredded, to garnish

For the base:

Plain flour 250g (9oz)

Bicarbonate of soda ½ rounded tsp

Salt ½ tsp

Buttermilk 284ml tub

1 Make the tomato paste for the topping first. Heat a small frying pan, add the oil, onion and garlic and cook over a low heat for 5 minutes until softened.

2 Add the tomatoes. Season well, adding sugar. Cook for 8–10 minutes until thickened to a paste.

3 Preheat the oven to 230°C/450°F/Gas 8. To make the base, sift the flour, bicarbonate of soda and salt into a large bowl. Pour in about 250ml (9fl oz) of the buttermilk and mix, using a fork, to make a soft but not too sticky dough. Add more of the buttermilk if you need to, or more flour if it gets too sticky.

4 Put the dough onto a work surface lightly dusted with flour. Knead briefly then divide it into four. Form each piece into a ball and place it on a greased heavy baking sheet. Flatten out with your knuckle each to a 15cm (6in) round.

5 Spread the tomato paste over each pizza, almost to the edge. Scatter with half the cheese, then the slices of sausage, the mushrooms, basil and, lastly, the rest of the cheese. Bake for 20 minutes. Serve warm with salad.

Asparagus with poached eggs

The English asparagus season only lasts a couple of months, so make the most of this delicacy by serving in different ways, such as with ham and eggs.

10 minutes preparation time
15 minutes cooking time
354 Kcal per portion
21.8g fat per portion of which
4.6g is saturated
4 servings

Asparagus spears
12, washed

Olive oil 4 tbsp

Rustic bread or ciabatta
4 large or 8 small slices

Parma or Serrano ham
6 slices, cut in half widthways

Wine or cider vinegar
a dash

Eggs 4 large free-range

Salt and freshly ground black pepper

1 Preheat the oven to 200°C/400°F/ Gas 6. Break the ends off the asparagus stalks where they naturally snap. Put the asparagus on a baking sheet, drizzle with 1 tbsp of the oil and rub it over the spears with your hands. Bake for 5 minutes.

2 Meanwhile, drizzle the rest of the oil over the slices of bread. When cooked, take the asparagus out of the oven and wrap half a piece of Parma ham around each stalk and put back on the baking sheet. Place the bread alongside. Bake for 10 minutes until the ham starts to go crispy, but do not overcook.

3 While the asparagus and bread are baking, bring a wide saucepan of water to the boil and add a dash of vinegar. Break in the eggs one at a time and let them poach over a gentle heat for 3–4 minutes, depending on how you like them.

4 Arrange the baked bread and roasted asparagus on four plates. Then carefully remove the poached eggs from the saucepan with a draining spoon and place on top. Sprinkle with salt and pepper.

Roasting asparagus gives a stronger, brighter taste than steaming or boiling. For more flavour, rub the bread with a cut clove of garlic or add garlic slivers to the roasting asparagus.

Cook's tips

•Adding vinegar to the egg poaching water helps the eggs to coagulate more quickly – white, cider or rice is preferable to malt vinegar.
•Wrap the asparagus in Serrano ham, which is easier to handle than Parma ham. Bacon tends to unwrap itself and is too fatty.

Macaroni cheese

Ideal for a weekday dinner, this version of macaroni cheese is quick, yet delicious.

15 minutes preparation time
25 minutes cooking time
457 Kcal per portion
14.3g fat per portion of which
7.9g is saturated
4 servings

Macaroni 250g (9oz)

Leek 1, washed, trimmed and cut into chunks

Broccoli 110g (4oz), cut into equal-sized florets

Streaky bacon 4 rashers (optional)

Semi-skimmed milk 350ml (12fl oz)

Plain flour 3 tbsp

English mustard 1 tsp ready-made

Extra-mature Cheddar cheese 110g (4oz) grated

Salt and freshly ground black pepper

Tomatoes 2, cut into wedges

Parmesan cheese freshly grated, 2 tbsp

1 Bring a large saucepan of salted water to the boil and add the pasta. Bring the water back to the boil, cook for 5 minutes and then add the leek and broccoli and cook for another 5 minutes.

2 Meanwhile, preheat the grill to hot and cook the streaky bacon rashers, if using. Pour the milk into a saucepan and, over a medium heat, whisk in the flour. Bring to the boil and keep whisking to make a smooth sauce. Simmer for 4 minutes and then add the mustard and half the Cheddar and season well.

3 Put a flameproof dish under the grill to heat up. Drain the pasta and vegetables well. Tip them back into the saucepan and gently stir in the cheese sauce. Spoon the mixture into the hot dish and sprinkle with the rest of the Cheddar.

4 Arrange the tomato wedges on top and snip the bacon, if using, with scissors, into small pieces, and tuck them into the sauce. Sprinkle with Parmesan and put the dish under the grill to brown the top. Serve hot with green vegetables or salad.

Cook's tips

•This is easy to make for vegetarians – just leave out the bacon and use the appropriate cheese.
•Adding vegetables to the pasta is a good way of 'hiding' vegetables for those in the family not so keen on them.
•Use an extra-mature Cheddar and you won't need to keep piling cheese in to get a good cheesy sauce.

Squash, bean & Stilton risotto

Rich and creamy with a fantastic colour, this combination of textures and flavours results in simple, modern, comfort food!

10 minutes preparation time
40 minutes cooking time
546 Kcal per portion
23.6g fat per portion of which
11.6g is saturated
4 servings
Suitable for vegetarians

Butternut squash 1, weighing about 900g (2lb)

Olive oil 2 tbsp

Butter 50g (2oz)

Onion 1, peeled and diced

Garlic 1 clove, peeled and crushed

Arborio (risotto) rice 250g (9oz)

Dry cider 150ml (¼ pint)

Vegetable stock 750ml (1¼ pints)

Frozen broad beans 150g (5oz)

Salt and freshly ground black pepper

Stilton cheese 75g (3oz)

Sage leaves 8, shredded

1 Preheat the oven to 200°C/400°F/ Gas 6. Cut the squash into about 8 big chunks, removing the seeds. Put the chunks in a roasting tin with 1 tbsp of oil and roast in the oven for 40 minutes, turning the pieces a couple of times during cooking. They should be softened and caramelised on the edges.

2 Meanwhile, heat the rest of the oil with the butter in a large saucepan. Add the onion and cook over a medium heat for 5 minutes. Stir in the garlic and rice and coat well in the butter for a couple of minutes. Pour in the cider, let it sizzle and, when it is almost absorbed, pour in about 200ml (7fl oz) of the stock.

3 Cook over a low heat until the stock is absorbed. Continue to add more stock in batches as it becomes absorbed into the rice. With the last addition of stock, add the broad beans as well.

4 Remove the skin from all but the 'best-looking' pieces of squash. Set these aside for the garnish. Mash the flesh from the rest roughly with a fork, in the roasting tin, and add it to the risotto with the saucepan juices. Check for seasoning and, when the rice is just cooked, break small chunks of Stilton over the top. Garnish with shredded sage leaves.

Cook's tip

•**Roast butternut squash is great served as an accompaniment to roast meat dishes. Squash can be peeled before cooking, but it's quicker to do it afterwards. Let it get really brown and sticky for the best flavour.**

Spring greens & plaice gratin

Plaice is delicate and best cooked simply, the spring greens do add colour, crunch and a fresh flavour to this dish.

15 minutes preparation time
45 minutes cooking time
481 Kcal per portion
28.9g fat per portion of which
15.2g is saturated
4 servings

Plaice fillets 8, skinned
Salt and freshly ground black pepper
White wine or dry cider 150ml (¼ pint)
Spring greens 250g (9oz), sliced
Butter 25g (1oz)
Double cream 142ml pot
Egg yolks 2
Nutmeg freshly grated
Breadcrumbs a good handful

1 Preheat the oven to 190°C/375°F/ Gas 5 and butter a shallow ovenproof dish. Lay the fish fillets out on the work surface, skinless side up. Season them well and then roll up from the tail end. Pack fairly tightly in the dish. Add the wine or cider, cover with foil and bake for 25–30 minutes.

2 Meanwhile, bring a large saucepan of salted water to the boil and add the greens, boiling them for 5 minutes. Drain well in a colander, gently pressing out the water. Tip onto a board and chop roughly, discarding any remaining thick stalks. Put the greens back in the saucepan on the heat, add the butter and stir for a minute. Set aside.

3 When the fish is cooked, pour the cooking liquid into a small frying pan and boil it for about 5 minutes until reduced to 100ml (3½fl oz). Put the foil back on the fish and keep it warm. Preheat the grill to medium.

4 Stir the cream into the fish stock and bring to the boil for another 5 minutes until reduced. Add a little of the cream sauce to the egg yolks and return this mixture to the sauce. Cook gently for a couple of minutes being careful not to overheat or the yolks could curdle, taste and season.

5 Scatter the greens over the plaice, grate a generous amount of nutmeg on top, then pour the sauce over and sprinkle with breadcrumbs. Put the dish under the grill to brown the top – watch it, as it doesn't take long. Serve with new potatoes and peas or green beans.

Cook's tips
•**Order the fish from a fishmonger or the supermarket, requesting they skin the fillets for you – they can probably do it more quickly.**
•**For an extra-special treat, put a slice of smoked salmon on the plaice fillet and roll it up inside. Or even more special – use sole fillets instead of plaice.**

This recipe could be made with any fish fillets. Thick pieces of cod, haddock or salmon – just put them in the dish, don't attempt to roll them. If you're not keen on spring greens, cook broccoli instead.

Plaice with a leek & bacon sauce

A light, colourful and easy-to-cook recipe, which makes the most of the seasonal ingredients available. It works well with most varieties of white fish.

2 minutes preparation time
10 minutes cooking time
347 Kcal per portion
24.1g fat per portion of which
13.6g is saturated
4 servings

Bacon 50g (2oz)

Leeks 2, washed, trimmed and sliced

Plain flour 25g (1oz)

Salt and freshly ground black pepper

Plaice fillets 4, skinned

Butter 25g (1oz)

Whipping or double cream 150ml (¼ pint)

Cook's tip

•**Always check fish fillets very carefully for bones before cooking them as finding a bone can make people wary and dissuade them from eating any fish, to the detriment of their diet.**

1 Heat a large, non-stick frying pan and dry-fry the bacon, turning regularly, until crisp. Remove from the pan and cut into small pieces.

2 Meanwhile, bring a saucepan of salted water to the boil and add the leeks. Cook for 3–5 minutes and then drain and refresh under cold running water and leave to drain once more.

3 Sprinkle the flour across a plate, add seasoning and coat the plaice on both sides.

4 In the frying pan, melt the butter and fry the fish for 2 minutes on each side, turning once. Remove the fish from the pan and keep warm on serving plates. Wipe out the pan.

5 Add the cream, bring to the boil and leave to simmer for 1–2 minutes to reduce. Then add the blanched leeks, mix together and season well. Spoon the leeks over the fish and sprinkle with the bacon bits. Serve with mashed potato and fresh asparagus or green beans.

Sea bream with herb mash

This recipe is good for entertaining as everything except grilling the fish can be done in advance. It looks stylish, but is really simple to create.

20 minutes preparation time
25 minutes cooking time
406 Kcal per portion
22.4g fat per portion of which
6g is saturated
4 servings

Potatoes 4, peeled and cut into chunks

Coriander seeds 1 tsp, lightly crushed

Olive oil 4 tbsp

Tomatoes 4 ripe but firm

Balsamic vinegar 1 tbsp

Whole green or black olives 8, sliced

Sugar a pinch (optional)

Sea bream fillets 4, weighing about 150g (5oz) each

Salt and freshly ground black pepper

Milk 6 tbsp

Butter 25g (1oz)

Chopped parsley 2 handfuls

Chopped chives a handful

Basil about 12 leaves, to garnish

1 Bring a saucepan of salted water to the boil, add the potatoes and cook for about 20 minutes until tender.

2 Meanwhile, put the coriander seeds in a small saucepan with 1 tbsp of the oil. Fry for a minute. Set aside.

3 Drop the tomatoes in with the boiling potatoes for about half a minute to loosen the skin, then cool them under cold running water and peel off the skin. Quarter and deseed the tomatoes, putting the seeds in a sieve over the saucepan that the coriander seeds are in, and press them gently to squeeze out the juices into the saucepan. Discard the tomato seeds. Dice the tomato flesh.

4 Heat the juices in the saucepan for a few minutes until they have reduced by half then add another 2 tbsp of the oil, the balsamic vinegar, diced tomatoes and olives.

5 Taste for acidity and seasoning, adding sugar if it needs sweetening. Put to one side.

6 To cook the fish, heat a non-stick griddle, grill or sturdy frying pan. Brush the rest of the oil on both sides of the fish, season the fillets well and cook for 3 minutes on each side. Gently heat the tomato vinaigrette to warm it through.

7 At the same time, drain the potatoes. Put them back in the saucepan over a low heat, add the milk and, when it bubbles, add the butter. Take off the heat and mash. Season and stir in the chopped herbs.

8 Spoon the herb mash onto hot plates, arrange the fish on top and spoon the tomato vinaigrette around the mash. Shred the basil leaves and sprinkle over the sauce. Grind pepper over the fish.

Cook's tip

•**Use any fish fillets that you fancy – sea bass, mullet or mackerel would be fine. Keep a look out for special offers at the fish counter, especially on the usually more expensive fish.**

Chicken & asparagus pie

Using ready-made pastry isn't considered to be 'cheating' these days and everyone loves a pastry-topped pie, so make them more often!

20 minutes preparation time
25 minutes cooking time
709 Kcal per portion
36.4g fat per portion of which
16.2g is saturated
4 servings
Suitable for freezing

Butter 25g (1oz)

Carrots 2, peeled and diced

Shallots 8, trimmed and halved

Button mushrooms 110g (4oz), wiped

Plain flour 25g (1oz)

Milk 450ml (¾ pint)

Asparagus 175g (6oz), trimmed and cut into short lengths

Cooked chicken 450g (1lb), cut into strips

Salt and freshly ground black pepper

Single cream 2 tbsp

Ready-to-roll puff pastry 375g sheet

Egg 1, beaten

1 Preheat the oven to 200°C/400°F/ Gas 6. Melt the butter in a large saucepan and sauté the carrots, shallots and mushrooms. Cook for 5 minutes and then stir in the flour and gradually add the milk, stirring until the sauce thickens, boils and becomes smooth.

2 In a separate saucepan, bring salted water to the boil, add the asparagus and cook for 3 minutes to blanch it. Drain and refresh under cold running water and then drain well again.

3 Add the chicken, asparagus, seasoning and cream to the sauce. Pour the mixture into a 1.25 litre (2 pint) pie dish.

4 Roll out the pastry to the same size as the dish, dampen the rim of the dish and cover with the pastry. Brush with the beaten egg.

5 Bake in the oven for 25 minutes until the pastry is golden brown. Serve with a baked potato.

This recipe makes good use of those thinner stalks of asparagus that would be tricky to eat with the fingers. Combining them with chicken creates a great flavour and an interesting contrast of textures in the pie filling.

Cook's tip
•**With the pastry offcuts make some jam tarts for tea time. Even if you only have enough pastry left for half a dozen, they are always a welcome treat.**

Lemon chicken & potato wedges

This recipe is a good alternative to the Sunday roast, especially if you have visitors, as it looks great and it's easy to double the ingredients for more people.

10 minutes preparation time
55 minutes cooking time
426 Kcal per portion
20.5g fat per portion of which
6.9g is saturated
4 servings

Potatoes 4, peeled and cut into wedges

Olive oil 3 tbsp

Lemons 2, 1 cut into 6 wedges and the other into 8 thin slices

Garlic 4 cloves, unpeeled

Handful of thyme or oregano sprigs

Chicken breasts 4, skin left on

Salt and freshly ground black pepper

Nutmeg freshly grated

Parma ham 4 slices

Chicken stock 150ml (¼ pint)

Crème fraîche 4 tbsp

1 Preheat the oven to 190°C/375°F/Gas 5 and put a large baking tray inside to heat up. Bring a saucepan of salted water to the boil, add the potato wedges and leave to simmer for 5 minutes. Drain the potatoes and then leave to dry for a few seconds in the saucepan.

2 Put 2 tbsp of oil on the hot baking sheet, add the potatoes and toss in the oil. Gently squeeze each lemon wedge over the potatoes and add them to the baking tray, along with the garlic cloves and herb sprigs. Roast near the bottom of the oven for about 50 minutes, turning them after 25 minutes and then once again to crisp and brown all over.

3 Meanwhile, put the chicken breasts in a roasting tin, rub the skin with the lemon ends and then season well with salt, pepper and nutmeg. Arrange a slice of ham on each piece of meat, ruching it to look attractive, and then put 2 lemon slices on top. Drizzle with 1 tbsp of oil. Put the chicken above the potato wedges in the oven and cook for 20 minutes, then pour the stock into the tin and cook for another 20 minutes.

4 Transfer the chicken to a hot platter. Pour the roasting tin juices into a small saucepan, bring to the boil and reduce to about 90ml (3fl oz). Whisk in the crème fraîche to make a thin creamy sauce. Spoon some sauce onto four hot dinner plates and place a chicken breast on top. Serve with the lemon-flavoured wedges, garlic cloves and some green vegetables.

Cook's tips

•If you want less fat in this recipe, take the skin off the chicken and don't add the crème fraîche to the sauce – it still tastes just delicious.

•The recipe works well with chicken leg portions too – cook them for 50 minutes rather than the 40 minutes given above.

Pesto chicken & roast potatoes

Making pesto sauce is easy, and it doesn't have to contain basil and pine nuts.
Try this variation using parsley and walnuts served with stir-fried chicken.

10 minutes preparation time
40 minutes cooking time
475 Kcal per portion
34.2g fat per portion of which
8.9g is saturated
4 servings

Potatoes 4, totalling
about 800g (1¾lb),
peeled and cut into cubes

Olive oil 8 tbsp

Chicken breasts 4,
skinned and cut into
finger-width strips

Crème fraîche 4 tbsp

For the pesto:
Flat-leaved parsley 50g
(2oz), thick stalks
removed

Walnuts 8 halves or 15g
(½oz), roughly chopped

Garlic 1 clove, peeled
and chopped

Salt ½ tsp

Parmesan cheese 3 tbsp
freshly grated

1 Preheat the oven to 200°C/400°F/
Gas 6 and heat a shallow roasting tin
or tray. Bring a saucepan of salted
water to the boil and add the
potatoes. Bring back to the boil, cook
for 5 minutes and drain well.

2 Spoon 2 tbsp of oil into the roasting
tin and toss in the potato cubes. Roast
for 40 minutes, turning them a few
times so they crisp and brown all over.

3 Meanwhile, make the pesto. Wash
the parsley and dry it gently in a tea
towel. Heat a non-stick frying pan, add
the walnuts and dry-fry until lightly
toasted. Put them in a small food
processor with the garlic, salt and
parsley leaves and pulse a few times
for a rough texture. Add the cheese
and 5 tbsp of the oil. Whizz once
again to blend the ingredients, but
not too smoothly.

4 Heat a wok or large frying pan,
pour in the remaining oil and add the
chicken strips in one layer. Cook for
2–3 minutes until the strips are brown
then turn over and cook for another
couple of minutes.

5 Add the crème fraîche and 3 tbsp
of the pesto and simmer for 5 minutes.
Add 2 tbsp more of pesto and serve
the chicken strips with the roast
potatoes and fresh vegetables.

Cook's tips

•**There should be about 4 tbsp of pesto
left. Put this in a ramekin dish or small
jar, cover the top with a little olive oil
and then cling film and store in the
fridge. It will keep for a week or more
and can be stirred into pasta or rice to
serve four people.**
•**Make pesto with mixtures of herbs
that you might have in the garden –
experiment with flavours. Use pine
nuts, hazelnuts or almonds.**

Lamb in cabbage fans

Here is a British version of dolmas – or stuffed vine leaves – made with a much tastier and more generous amount of filling.

10 minutes preparation time
40 minutes cooking time
346 Kcal per portion
21.7g fat per portion of which
9.6g is saturated
6 servings
Suitable for freezing

Butter 50g (2oz)

Onion, red or white 1, peeled and chopped

Basmati or long grain rice 110g (4oz)

Stock cube 1 lamb, saffron rice or vegetable flavour

Savoy cabbage leaves 12 outer leaves (see Cook's Tips), washed

Minced lamb 450g (1lb)

Chopped parsley a good handful, plus extra for serving (optional)

Ground cinnamon 1 tsp

Ground cumin 1 tsp

Salt and freshly ground black pepper

Pine nuts 4 tbsp, toasted

Chopped tomatoes 400g can

1 Melt half the butter in a large frying pan with a lid. Add the onion and cook for a few minutes. Stir in the rice and cook for another couple of minutes. Make the stock cube up to 600ml (1 pint) with boiling water. Pour in half the stock to just cover the rice, then put a lid on the pan and leave over a low heat for 10 minutes, stirring occasionally, until the rice is just tender and the stock absorbed. Leave in the pan to cool a little.

2 Meanwhile, bring a large saucepan of salted water to the boil and add the cabbage leaves, 6 at a time, and leave to simmer for 3 minutes. Take them out, cool under cold running water and drain. Cut out the tough centre stalk from each leaf and lay the leaves on the work surface, inside up, with the top of the leaf facing you.

3 Add the minced lamb, parsley, spices, seasoning and 3 tbsp of pine nuts to the rice in the frying pan. Mix in well – with your hand is the best way – squeezing everything together. Divide the mixture equally between the cabbage leaves, putting it at the top of the leaf end. Fold the left side of the leaf over the filling, then the right side and, finally, roll up the leaves to look like parcels.

4 Pour the can of tomatoes into a shallow but large ovenproof dish (or use two gratin dishes) then pack in the parcels fairly tightly. Pour over the rest of the stock and dot each parcel with the remaining butter. Cover the dish with foil and bake for 40 minutes.

5 Remove from the oven and take off the foil. Sprinkle over the reserved pine nuts and more parsley if you like. Serve straight from the dish, with some new potatoes and green beans.

Cook's tips

• To get **12 dark green, good-size leaves you may need to buy 2 Savoy cabbages. Use the leftover hearts shredded in stir-fries or as a vegetable side dish. They will keep in a polybag in the fridge for a week.**
• **Cut most of the stalk out of each leaf – it will mean they are almost cut in half but the filling will not stray out.**

Spring herb roast lamb

New season lamb is lovely and tender but it can also be pricey in early spring, so wait until the price drops a little before you indulge in this delicious roast.

20 minutes preparation time
1 hour 40 minutes cooking time
378 Kcal per portion
24.4g fat per portion of which
10.7g is saturated
6 servings

Anchovies 50g can

Garlic 3 fat cloves, peeled and chopped

Capers 2 tbsp, rinsed

Chopped parsley 3 tbsp

Lemon 1, finely grated rind

Breadcrumbs 3 tbsp

Leg of lamb 2kg (4lb 8oz) on the bone or 1kg (2lb 4oz) boned and rolled

Rosemary a few long sprigs

Thyme a handful

Olive oil 1 tbsp

Freshly ground black pepper

1 Preheat the oven to 220°C/425°F/ Gas 7. Drain the oil from the anchovy can into a small bowl. Roughly chop the anchovies and add to the oil with the garlic, capers, parsley, lemon rind and breadcrumbs to make a paste.

2 Cut through the lamb at about 2.5cm (1in) intervals, almost to the bone, and push the paste down into the slashes.

3 Put the lamb on top of the herbs in a roasting tin. Drizzle with oil and season with pepper. Roast for 20 minutes then turn down the heat to 190°C/375°F/Gas 5 and cook for another 1 hour and 20 minutes for the lamb on the bone. For boned lamb, cook for 20 minutes at the high temperature and then for 40 minutes at the lower temperature.

4 When cooked, put the lamb on a hot serving platter. Leave loosely covered with foil for 10 minutes to rest. Discard the sprigs of rosemary and use the roasting tin juices to make gravy (see Cook's Tips). Serve with roast potatoes, carrots and parsnips together with wedges of spring cabbage (for Savoy cabbage hearts, see Cook's Tips, page 34).

Cook's tips

- Check the weight of the lamb and work out the cooking time to suit your tastes (20 minutes per 450g/1lb for rare, 25 for medium, 30 for well done, plus an extra 20 minutes).
- Allow 1 potato, half a medium parsnip and 1 carrot per person. Par-boil the vegetables and roast below the meat for about an hour.
- Add sherry or red wine to the roasting tin juices and some lamb stock. Thicken with cornflour or gravy granules.

Sausage & bean pasta

Buy your favourite sausages and skin them for making this tasty pasta dish, or use good-quality sausagemeat, which makes a change from beef or lamb.

10 minutes preparation time
25 minutes cooking time
632 Kcal per portion
28.4g fat per portion of which
9.2g is saturated
4 servings
Suitable for freezing

Sausages 450g (1lb), good quality

Olive oil 2 tbsp

Onion 1 small, peeled and chopped

Garlic 1 clove, peeled and chopped

Chopped tomatoes 2 x 400g cans

Basil about 25g (1oz), roughly torn except for 4 sprigs (optional)

Pasta shells 300g (11oz)

Runner beans 110g (4oz) finely sliced

Parmesan cheese freshly grated, 2 tbsp, plus extra for serving

1 Skin the sausages and break each one into 7–8 pieces. Heat 1 tbsp of oil in a frying pan, add the chunks of sausage and fry for 5 minutes. Add the onion and garlic and cook for another 5 minutes, stirring occasionally.

2 Stir in the tomatoes and add half the basil. Simmer for about 15 minutes until thickened.

3 Meanwhile, bring a large, lidded saucepan of salted water to the boil, add the pasta and cook for 10–12 minutes, adding the beans after 8 minutes, cooking until pasta and beans are just tender. Drain well, then toss in remaining oil and the Parmesan cheese.

4 Spoon the pasta with the beans into four warmed shallow bowls. Check the sausagemeat sauce for seasoning and add the rest of the basil – keeping back 4 sprigs for garnish, if you like. Spoon the sauce over the pasta and serve with extra freshly grated Parmesan.

Cook's tips

•**Don't roll the sausagemeat into balls; just keep it in odd-shaped chunks – it looks and tastes even better that way.**
•**Use small chunks of chicken, pork or beef instead of sausages, served with this sauce.**

Savoury pancake stack

Using the most traditional of spring fare — the pancake — here is an unusual and delicious dish, which looks just as impressive as it tastes.

20 minutes preparation time
30 minutes cooking time
551 Kcal per portion
31.6g fat per portion of which
14.2g is saturated
4 servings
Pancakes are suitable for freezing

For the pancakes:
Plain flour 125g (4½oz)
Egg 1 large
Milk 300ml (½ pint)
Sunflower oil 2 tbsp for cooking

For the filling:
Thick bacon 200g (7oz), de-rinded and diced
Onion 1, peeled and diced
Cup mushrooms 150g (5oz), wiped and chopped
Salt and freshly ground black pepper
Chopped parsley 5 tbsp

For the sauce:
Butter 40g (1½oz)
Plain flour 40g (1½oz)
Milk 450ml (¾ pint)
Coarse-grain mustard 1 tbsp
Mature Cheddar cheese 50g (2oz), grated

1 To make the pancakes, put the flour into a large bowl and add the egg and half the milk. Mix well with a hand mixer until it is bubbly. Stir in the rest of the milk.

2 Heat an 18–20cm (7–8in) shallow frying pan, add a few drops of oil and, when hot, pour in enough batter, tilting the pan to coat the base evenly. Cook until the pancake browns underneath, then turn it over using a palette knife and cook for another half a minute. Slide the pancake out onto a plate. Make 8 pancakes, separating each with kitchen paper. Set aside, keeping warm (see Cook's Tips).

3 Then make the filling. Heat a frying pan and fry the bacon and onion for 5 minutes. Add the mushrooms, cook for 5 minutes and season well. Preheat the oven to 200°C/400°F/Gas 6.

4 To make the sauce, melt the butter in a small saucepan, add the flour and cook the paste for a minute. Gradually beat in the milk. Bring to the boil, stirring for a thick smooth sauce. Stir in the mustard and half the cheese. Then add half of the sauce to the mushroom mixture together with the chopped parsley.

5 Place 1 pancake on a buttered ovenproof plate or baking sheet. Spread with some of the mushroom filling, put another pancake on top and continue spreading and layering, ending with a pancake. Sprinkle the rest of the cheese on top. Cover loosely with foil.

6 Bake for 10 minutes to heat through, then remove the foil to brown the cheese a little for about 5 minutes. Reheat the remaining sauce, adding a little more milk or water to thin it down if you like. Cut the pancake stack into wedges, pour over the sauce and serve with heaps of freshly cooked vegetables.

Cook's tips

• Keep the pancakes hot by placing them on a plate, covering with foil and setting over a saucepan of simmering water. Or put the covered plate in the oven at 150°C/300°F/Gas 2.
• Add leftover cooked chicken or ham to the filling instead of bacon, or cut out the meat, adding extra mushrooms and a small can of sweetcorn.

Bacon and mushroom is a lovely combination of textures and flavours. Try substituting leeks for the mushrooms. An alternative would be to use layers of mince and spinach.

Leicester pork chops

Add a bit of excitement to pork chops with this mixed cheesy stuffing.
Serve with home-made chunky chips cooked in the oven on the shelf below.

15 minutes preparation time
45 minutes cooking time
510 Kcal per portion
35.5g fat per portion of which
17.4g is saturated
4 servings

Red Leicester cheese
50g (2oz), grated
Low fat soft cheese 75g
(3oz)
Fresh breadcrumbs 25g
(1oz)
Horseradish sauce 1 tbsp
Chopped parsley 2 tsp
Pork chops 4 x 150g
(5oz)
Butter 25g (1oz)
Sherry 3 tbsp
Double cream 3 tbsp

1 Preheat the oven to 190°C/375°F/ Gas 5. Mix together the cheeses, breadcrumbs, horseradish and parsley. Cut a deep pocket in the flesh of each chop and fill with the cheese mixture.

2 Melt the butter in a roasting tin. Add the chops and fry to brown on both sides. Cover with foil and bake in the oven for 30 minutes. Uncover and cook for a further 10 minutes.

3 Remove the tin from the oven, take out the chops and keep them warm. Add the sherry to the tin, scrape up any sediment and mix in well. Bring to the boil on the hob and cook until reduced to a syrup. Remove from the heat and stir in the cream. Spoon the creamy sauce over the chops and serve with roasted chunky chips (see Cook's Tips).

Cook's tips
•**Cut potatoes into chunky chips and cook, coated in a few tablespoons of oil, on a baking sheet near the bottom of the oven for 40–50 minutes, turning them over occasionally.**
•**You could add Cheddar or Stilton to the stuffing instead of Red Leicester.**

Spicy beef & orange casserole

Slow cooking in this North African style gives the meat a slightly sweet flavour and more tender texture. It makes a tasty change from a red wine sauce.

25 minutes preparation time
2 hours cooking time
385 Kcal per portion
17.9g fat per portion of which
6.3g is saturated
4 servings
Suitable for freezing

Ground ginger ½ tsp
Ground cinnamon ½ tsp
Ground cloves ½ tsp
Ground nutmeg ½ tsp
Mixed spice 1 tsp
Salt and freshly ground black pepper
Plain flour 2 tbsp
Lean stewing steak 450g (1lb), cubed
Butter 25g (1oz)
Onion 1, peeled and sliced
Celery 4 sticks, sliced
Oranges 2, grated rind and segmented fruit
Orange juice 450ml (¾ pint)
Chopped walnuts 3 tbsp

Cook's tips

•**Use orange juice from a carton unless you have lots of the fresh fruit available for squeezing.**
•**This recipe would work well with lamb or pork.**
•**If freezing, leave out the orange segments and walnuts and add them when reheating.**

1 Preheat the oven to 180°C/350°F/ Gas 4. In a large bowl, mix all the spices plus seasoning with the flour. Add the beef and coat it lightly all over with the seasoned flour.

2 Melt the butter in a large, lidded flameproof casserole and add the beef, reserving the excess flour. Cook until browned all over. Remove the meat and set aside.

3 Add the onion and celery to the casserole and cook for 3 minutes. Stir in the remaining flour and orange rind and cook for a further minute.

4 Gradually stir in the orange juice and bring to the boil, stirring constantly. Cook for 1 minute.

5 Add the beef, cover, place in the oven and cook for 1½ hours.

6 Stir in the orange segments and walnuts and return to the oven for a further 30 minutes. Serve with rice and steamed vegetables.

Minced beef filo parcels

These parcels filled with beef and vegetables are not difficult to make but look impressive and can be served as party snacks as well as for a main meal.

15 minutes preparation time
45 minutes cooking time
136 Kcal per parcel
5.2g fat per portion of which
2.2g is saturated
Makes 20 parcels

Lean minced beef 450g (1lb)

Spring onions 2, trimmed and finely chopped

Button mushrooms 225g (8oz), chopped

Sweetcorn 110g can

Red wine 150ml (¼ pint)

Tomato purée 1 tbsp

Bacon 110g (4oz), finely chopped

Dried mixed herbs 1 tsp

Garlic 1 clove, crushed

Spinach 225g (8oz), cooked, drained and chopped

Salt and freshly ground black pepper

Butter 25g (1oz), melted

Filo pastry 400g packet

1 Dry-fry the minced beef and spring onions in a large, non-stick, lidded saucepan for 5 minutes. Add the mushrooms, sweetcorn, wine, tomato purée, bacon, herbs and garlic. Cover and cook for 20 minutes.

2 Add the spinach, season and cook for a further 5 minutes, uncovered. Leave to cool and preheat the oven to 180°C/350°F/Gas 4.

3 In a small saucepan gently melt the butter. Cut the filo sheets into 60 x 15cm (6in) squares and then for each parcel lay 3 squares of filo pastry on top of each other to make a 12-pointed star, brushing with butter between each layer.

4 Place 2 tbsp of the beef mixture into the centre of each filo 'star' and gather up to make a parcel. Repeat until all the remaining filo pastry and filling are used up.

5 Place the parcels on a lined baking sheet and brush each one with melted butter. Bake for 15–20 minutes until golden brown. Serve with steamed Savoy cabbage and cauliflower.

Cook's tips
•Work quickly when using filo pastry or it dries out and cracks.
•This recipe idea is great for using up leftover cooked meat. Just mince it or chop it finely and add cooked vegetables and/or frozen peas and some cold gravy.

Filo pastry is easy to shape and these minced beef 'money bags' will cause a real stir among your guests! You could experiment with different fillings and make other shapes such as triangles.

Rhubarb & custard ice cream

Celebrate the wonderful taste of fresh rhubarb with this ice cream. It's simple to make and perfect for an afternoon treat when the days start to get warmer.

35 minutes preparation time plus freezing
437 Kcal per portion
35.7g fat per portion of which
21.2g is saturated
8 servings
Suitable for freezing
Suitable for vegetarians

Double cream 500ml pot

Orange 1, pared rind and juice

Egg yolks 4

Light muscovado sugar 175g (6oz)

Greek natural yogurt 200g tub

Rhubarb 500g (1lb 2oz) trimmed weight, cut into chunks

Fruity teabread 1–2 thin slices, toasted for serving

Icing sugar and cinnamon for sifting (optional)

Cook's tips

•**If you have an ice cream maker, just put the rhubarb custard in and use as directed. It's less hassle than to keep remembering to whisk it every few hours.**
•**The ice cream will keep for up to 2 months in the freezer.**

1 Heat the cream with the pared orange rind in a saucepan over a gentle heat until it just comes to the boil. Leave to infuse for 5 minutes.

2 Meanwhile, in a large bowl whisk the egg yolks and 110g (4oz) of the sugar until thickened and light in colour. Add a little of the warmed cream mixture, stir well and then add the rest of the cream mixture.

3 Pour the mixture back into the saucepan and stir continuously over a gentle heat until the custard is thick enough to coat the back of a spoon (about 5 minutes). Don't let it boil or the egg yolks may curdle.

4 Strain the custard back into the bowl and cover closely with cling film. Leave to cool, discard the orange parings, stir in the yogurt and then chill the mixture.

5 Meanwhile, put the rhubarb in a saucepan with the juice from the orange (6–8 tbsp) and the rest of the sugar. Cover and cook gently for 6–7 minutes until the fruit is tender. Tip the rhubarb into a sieve set over a large measuring jug or bowl. Leave like this for 10 minutes or so, to let the juices drain through. You should have about 200ml (7fl oz) juice. Reserve this for the sauce.

6 Mash the rhubarb roughly with a fork and, when cold, stir it into the custard. Pour into a plastic container and freeze until almost solid (4–5 hours). Break up well with a fork or, better still, an electric hand mixer. Refreeze until almost solid (about a further 4 hours), then break up again so the ice cream is smooth, and freeze once more.

7 Taste the reserved rhubarb juice and add more sugar if it's not sweet enough. Pour the juice into a small saucepan, bring to the boil and reduce for about 10 minutes until it starts to become syrupy.

8 Transfer the ice cream from the freezer to the fridge about 40 minutes before serving to soften it. Put 2–3 small scoops into individual glasses, spoon over the warm sauce and serve with slices of toasted fruity teabread (sift icing sugar and cinnamon over the teabread if you like).

Rhubarb & raspberry crumble

Everyone loves crumble, so this family pud will always go down a treat.
The colours and flavours work wonderfully well together.

15 minutes preparation time
30 minutes cooking time
334 Kcal per portion
17g fat per portion of which
7g is saturated
4 servings
Suitable for vegetarians

Plain flour 75g (3oz)

Butter 50g (2oz)

Ground almonds 25g
(1oz)

Demerara sugar 6 tbsp

Rhubarb 500g (1lb 2oz)
trimmed weight, cut into
2.5cm (1in) chunks

Raspberries 175g (6oz),
fresh or frozen

Flaked almonds 2 tbsp

Cook's tip

•**The raspberries reduce
during cooking but they
are a good addition as
they help to soften the
sometimes 'sharp edge'
of rhubarb.**

1 Preheat the oven to 190°C/375°F/
Gas 5. Tip the flour into a mixing
bowl. Add slivers of butter and then,
using your fingertips, rub it in until it
looks like breadcrumbs. Stir in the
ground almonds and 2 tbsp of sugar.

2 Put half the rhubarb in an
ovenproof dish, scatter 2 tbsp sugar
and the raspberries over, then add
the rest of the rhubarb and another
tbsp of sugar.

3 Spoon the crumble topping over,
piling it high to cover the fruit. Put the
dish on a baking sheet. Sprinkle with
the remaining sugar and the flaked
almonds. Bake for 30 minutes until the
topping is golden and the fruit
softened and just oozing from under
the crumble. Serve warm or cold with
custard, cream or ice cream.

Coconut rice pudding

Comfort food with added spice! This pudding is perfect to make if you have lots of milk to use up. It is delicious cold too.

5 minutes preparation time
35 minutes cooking time
210 Kcal per portion
5.9g fat per portion of which
3.8g is saturated
4 servings
Suitable for vegetarians

Milk 900ml (1½ pints)
Coconut milk 3 tbsp
Ground cinnamon ½ tsp
Ground cloves ½ tsp
Pudding rice 75g (3oz)
Light/dark muscovado sugar 25g (1oz)
Sliced pistachio nuts to serve

1 Place the milk, coconut milk and spices in a saucepan and heat.

2 Stir in the rice and sugar and bring to the boil. Leave to simmer for 30 minutes, stirring occasionally, until the rice has thickened and cooked.

3 Serve hot or cold sprinkled with the sliced pistachio nuts.

Cook's tip
•A swirl of raspberry or strawberry purée would make a very pretty alternative topping for the rice pudding.

Pineapple upside-down pudding

When was the last time you made this pudding? Back in fashion, it's light, colourful and fruity and whipped up in no time – so go on, enjoy it!

10 minutes preparation time
35 minutes cooking time
349 Kcal per portion
17g fat per portion of which
10.1g is saturated
6 servings
Suitable for vegetarians

Golden syrup 4 tbsp
Pineapple rings 227g can of 4, drained
Glacé cherries 5, halved
Butter 110g (4oz), softened
Caster sugar 110g (4oz)
Eggs 2
Self-raising flour 110g (4oz), sifted

1 Preheat the oven to 180°C/350°F/ Gas 4. Grease and base line a 20cm (8in) sandwich tin. Spoon in the golden syrup and arrange the pineapple rings and 9 glacé cherry halves in it (1 in each ring, 1 in the centre and 4 around the edge, 1 between each ring). Pop in the glacé cherries cut side up so that when the finished pudding is turned out, it is the outside of the cherry that you see.

2 Cream together the butter and sugar until light and fluffy, add the eggs one at time with a little of the flour, then fold in the rest of the flour.

3 Spread the mixture evenly over the pineapple. Bake for about 35 minutes until just firm and golden. Leave the pudding in the tin for a few minutes then turn out and serve hot or cold with custard or cream.

Ginger balances the sweetness of pineapple very well. Add ground ginger to the sponge and use stem ginger slices on the base in addition to the pineapple. You could also pour in some of the syrup from the jar.

Cook's tips

- Soften the golden syrup by putting the open tin in the oven while it heats up.
- Add orange or lemon rind and juice to the sponge mixture.
- Add 2 tbsp cocoa powder blended with 2 tbsp hot water to the sponge mixture to make a chocolate pudding. Use pineapple or canned pears.

Fruity triple chocolate squares

This is an easy, no-bake recipe that children will love to make. Wrap a few squares in coloured tissue paper and give to loved ones for Easter.

10 minutes preparation time
2 minutes cooking time plus chilling
223 Kcal per square
14g fat per square of which
6.9g is saturated
Makes 16 squares
Suitable for freezing
Suitable for vegetarians

Butter 110g (4oz)

Plain chocolate 110g (4oz), broken into squares

Chocolate digestive biscuits 300g pack

Dried ready-to-eat apricots 75g (3oz), chopped

Dried cranberries 25g (1oz)

White chocolate 100g bar, roughly chopped

Cook's tips

• **These squares will keep for a week wrapped in foil in the fridge or up to 3 months in the freezer.**
• **Use any dried fruits, in any proportion you fancy.**

1 Line an 18cm (7in) square baking tin with cling film.

2 Put the butter and plain chocolate in a large bowl. Then microwave on full power for 1–2 minutes until the butter starts to melt or melt together in a bowl set over simmering water in a pan. Stir to blend them.

3 Put the biscuits in a strong polybag and, with your fist or a rolling pin, crush them to a coarse crumb. Add the crumbs to the bowl of melted butter and chocolate along with the dried fruits and chopped white chocolate. Mix well.

4 Spoon the mixture into the prepared tin, smoothing it down with the back of a spoon. Put in the fridge for at least 1 hour to firm. Take out of the tin and cut into 16 squares.

Easter biscuits

Traditionally, Easter biscuits are made with currants but this version is made with wild blueberries. Watch out though – one mouthful and you'll be hooked!

15 minutes preparation time plus chilling
18 minutes cooking time
81 Kcal per biscuit
4.1g fat per biscuit of which
2.5g is saturated
Makes 24–6 biscuits
Dough is suitable for freezing
Suitable for vegetarians

Plain flour 175g (6oz)

Mixed spice 1 tsp

Butter 110g (4oz)

Caster sugar 110g (4oz), plus extra for sprinkling

Lemon 1, grated rind

Wild blueberries 75g (3oz) (see Cook's Tips)

Egg 1, beaten

1 Sift the flour and spice into a large bowl. Add slivers of butter and then rub it in with your fingertips. Stir in the sugar, lemon rind and blueberries and then add the egg and mix to a firm dough.

2 Knead the dough briefly on a lightly floured surface and shape into a sausage about 20cm (8in) long and about 5cm (2in) wide. Wrap in cling film and chill in the fridge for an hour or in the freezer for half an hour.

3 Preheat the oven to 180°C/350°F/ Gas 4 and lightly grease a large baking sheet. Unwrap the chilled dough and cut into 5mm (¼in) thick slices. Put them on the baking sheet, spaced a little apart.

4 Bake the biscuits for 15–18 minutes until they are pale golden in colour. Cool on the baking sheet for a few minutes, sprinkle with a little caster sugar and then transfer the biscuits to a wire rack to cool.

Cook's tips

•The wild blueberries in this recipe are semi-dried and they are available in tubs in the same fixture in the supermarket as the dried fruits.
•Use currants or add orange rind if you like.
•For a more fancy biscuit, roll out the dough and cut with a shaped cutter.

Easter teabread

A quick version of simnel cake, this teabread is perfect with a hot cuppa after an Easter Sunday stroll.

20 minutes preparation time
1 hour cooking time
236 Kcal per slice
10.7g fat per slice of which
5.7g is saturated
Cuts into 12 slices
Suitable for freezing
Suitable for vegetarians

Plain flour 250g (9oz)

Baking powder 1 tsp

Bicarbonate of soda
1 tsp

Mixed spice 1 tsp

Butter 125g (4½oz)

Light muscovado sugar
110g (4oz)

Mixed dried fruit 250g
(9oz)

Milk 150ml (¼ pint)

Marzipan 150g (5oz)

Apricot jam 1 tbsp

1 Preheat the oven to 180°C/350°F/ Gas 4 and grease and line a 1kg (2lb 4oz) loaf tin with baking parchment.

2 Sift the flour, baking powder, bicarbonate of soda and spice into a large bowl. Add slivers of butter and then rub it in until it resembles fine breadcrumbs. Stir in the sugar and dried fruit. Add the milk and mix to a soft consistency.

3 Spoon half the mixture into the tin. Pull off small chunks of marzipan and make a layer of them over the cake mixture, but not right to the edges. Spoon over the rest of the cake mixture, smoothing the surface.

4 Bake for an hour until well risen and firm to the touch. Cover with foil for the last 15 minutes, if necessary. Cool in the tin for 10 minutes then run a knife round the edge, in case any marzipan has stuck to the tin, remove the loaf and put on a rack.

5 Heat the jam with 1 tbsp of water until just boiling, mix well and then brush the glaze over the warm loaf. Leave the loaf to cool. Slice into 12 pieces for serving.

This teabread freezes well for up to 3 months – so you can plan ahead for Easter. Wrap the loaf in cling film and foil and then seal and label. Loosen the wrappings before thawing.

Cook's tips

•**The usual skewer testing method for fruit cake does not work here because of the sticky marzipan.**
•**For the tastiest results, use good-quality dried fruit (or try some of the more exotic dried fruits) and ready-made golden or white marzipan. Cut the cherries into quarters with scissors.**

summer

Chilled cucumber & almond soup

This unusual-sounding starter is well worth trying, especially when served cold. It is perfect for a dinner party on a sultry summer's evening.

10 minutes preparation time
20 minutes cooking time plus chilling
184 Kcal per portion
14.8g fat per portion of which
2.6g is saturated
4 servings

Olive oil 2 tbsp

Spanish onion 1, finely chopped

Garlic 2 cloves, crushed

Bay leaf 1

Cucumber 1 large, peeled and chopped

Chicken stock 600ml (1 pint), cold

Ground almonds 50g (2oz)

Greek natural yogurt 6 tbsp

Salt and freshly ground black pepper

Cucumber slices, fennel leaves and ice cubes to serve

1 Heat the oil in a saucepan and gently fry the onion and garlic with the bay leaf for 10 minutes until soft but not browned.

2 Stir in the cucumber and pour over the stock. Bring to the boil, cover and simmer gently for 10 minutes. Remove from the heat and set aside to cool. Discard the bay leaf.

3 Transfer to a food processor and blend for a few seconds until smooth. Stir in the ground almonds and yogurt to thicken, and then season to taste. Pour into a jug, cover and chill. Serve in bowls with sliced cucumber, fennel leaves and ice cubes to float on top of the soup.

Cook's tips
•**For a vegetarian version, use vegetable stock. Replace the Greek yogurt with low fat natural yogurt for a lower fat version.**
•**If taking on a picnic, transport in a chilled vacuum flask and serve in mugs.**

Watercress & herb soup

The peppery taste of watercress makes for a delicious starter that is guaranteed to set your tastebuds tingling.

5 minutes preparation time
25 minutes cooking time
182 Kcal per portion
12.2g fat per portion of which
7.5g is saturated
6 servings
Suitable for freezing
Suitable for vegetarians

Butter 40g (1½oz)

Onion 1, peeled and chopped

Watercress 2 bunches, trimmed and chopped

Plain flour 40g (1½oz)

Milk 600ml (1 pint)

Vegetable stock 450ml (¾ pint)

Parsley 1 tbsp

Dill 1 tbsp

Chives 1 tbsp

Single cream 150ml (¼ pint)

Salt and freshly ground black pepper

Cook's tip
•**As an alternative, try replacing the watercress with half rocket and half baby spinach leaves.**

1 Melt the butter in a large pan and cook the onion for 3–4 minutes. Add the watercress and cook for a further 2–3 minutes.

2 Stir in the flour and cook for another minute. Remove from the heat and gradually stir in the milk and stock. Bring to the boil, stirring continuously, until thickened.

3 Add the herbs and simmer for another 15 minutes.

4 Cool slightly and then purée in a blender or food processor, in batches if necessary. Cool and chill. Stir in half the cream and season. Alternatively, return the purée to the saucepan and heat, but do not allow to boil, before stirring in half the cream. Serve chilled or warm, ladled into individual bowls with an added swirl of cream.

Mushrooms à la Greque

Here is a wonderfully simple yet tasty starter that makes the most of the meaty texture of mushrooms.

10 minutes preparation time
5 minutes cooking time plus chilling
109 Kcal per portion
7.8g fat per portion of which
1.1g is saturated
4 servings
Suitable for vegetarians

Baby button mushrooms 225g (8oz), wiped

Open cup mushrooms 225g (8oz), wiped

Vegetable stock 300ml (½ pint)

Bay leaves 2

Chopped tomatoes with garlic 400g can

Olive oil 2 tbsp

Ground cumin ½ tsp

Dry white wine 4 tbsp

Salt and freshly ground black pepper

Chopped flat-leaved parsley 4 tbsp

Pitted black olives in brine 50g (2oz), drained and roughly chopped

Cook's tips
• **Experiment with different varieties of mushrooms. There are so many to choose from and each has a subtly different flavour.**
• **For a more intense flavour, use unpitted black olives, either whole or – if you've time to spare – stoned and chopped.**

1 Wipe the mushrooms. Place the baby button mushrooms in a saucepan. Thickly slice the open cup mushrooms and add to the saucepan along with the stock and bay leaves. Bring to the boil, cover and simmer for 5 minutes until just tender. Remove from the heat and allow to cool. If you like, you can use the drained cooking liquid as a stock for soups or casseroles.

2 Drain the mushrooms and discard the bay leaves. Carefully mix in the tomatoes, olive oil, cumin, wine and seasoning. Cover the mixture and chill for at least an hour.

3 To serve, arrange on individual plates and sprinkle each portion with chopped parsley and a few olives.

Layered crunchy salad

This is a colourful and different way to serve a selection of salad vegetables, making an attractive dish to grace any table.

20 minutes preparation time
10 minutes cooking time plus chilling
274 Kcal per portion
14.2g fat per portion of which
2.7g is saturated
4 servings
Suitable for vegetarians

Eggs 4

Red pepper 1 small

Orange pepper 1 small

Red onion 1 small

Carrot 1

Ripe tomatoes 2

Radicchio lettuce or a few leaves of another red lettuce such as lollo rosso 1 small head

Sweetcorn kernels 325g can, drained

Red wine vinegar 1 tbsp

Olive oil 2 tbsp

Clear honey 2 tsp

Salt and freshly ground black pepper

Smoked paprika ½ tsp

1 Place the eggs in a small saucepan and cover with water. Bring to the boil and simmer gently for 8–10 minutes or until cooked to your liking – you do need the yolks to be quite firm for slicing. Drain and cool under cold running water. Set aside.

2 Halve and deseed the peppers and cut into thin strips. Peel and finely slice or chop the red onion. Peel and grate the carrot or cut into thin strips. Wash and thinly slice the tomatoes. Discard any damaged outer leaves from the lettuce, wash and shake dry. Then cut into thin shreds.

3 Line the base of a 1.25 litre (2 pint) pudding basin with a circle of baking parchment. Peel the eggs, cut into thin slices and place in the base of the pudding basin. Now layer up the vegetables in any order you like, packing them down well, until the basin is full.

4 Mix together the vinegar, oil, honey and seasoning and spoon over the top of the basin. Place a plate on top and weigh it down with a 450g (1lb) weight or a can of beans, etc. Place in the fridge for 1 hour.

5 To serve, remove the weight, invert the basin onto a serving plate and carefully lift off the basin. Season with black pepper and dust with paprika.

Cook's tip
•**To make a non-vegetarian salad for a main meal, add flaked tuna, peeled prawns, strips of cooked chicken or ham to this basic recipe.**

Grilled goat's cheese salad

A flavoursome trio of zesty orange, tangy goat's cheese and earthy beetroot. For the subtlest combination, use beetroot in natural juice.

20 minutes preparation time
2 minutes cooking time
500 Kcal per portion
34.5g fat per portion of which
19.9g is saturated
4 servings
Suitable for vegetarians

Oranges 4 large

Firm goat's cheese 4 x 110g (4oz) pieces

Bistro salad 150g bag of lamb's lettuce, baby red chard and beetroot strips

Cooked beetroot in natural juice 200g pack, drained

Wholegrain mustard 1 tbsp

Clear honey 1 tsp

Olive oil 2 tbsp

Salt and freshly ground black pepper

1 Slice the tops and bottoms from the oranges. Using a small, sharp knife, slice off the skin taking away as much of the pith as possible. Holding each orange over a bowl, slice in between the segments to release the flesh and juice into the bowl. Set aside.

2 Preheat the grill to a hot setting. Line the grill tray with foil. Arrange the cheese on the foil. Cook under the grill for about 2 minutes until lightly golden and slightly melting.

3 Arrange the salad leaves on four serving plates. Cut the cooked beetroot into thin strips. Drain the orange segments, reserving the juice, and arrange over the leaves, then sprinkle the beetroot on top. Top the salad with the goat's cheese, cut in half if preferred.

4 Blend the mustard, honey and oil with the orange juice. Season the dressing and spoon over the salad just prior to serving.

The range of flavours, textures and colours makes this salad a real treat. Soft goat's cheese melts in the mouth, the lettuce provides crispness and the orange bursts with juice.

Cook's tip
•**Try replacing the orange segments with sliced figs brushed with honey and then grilled.**

Fruity Greek salad

When peaches are at their most juicy and ripe, this is an ideal way to serve them as their sweetness complements the slightly acidic feta cheese.

20 minutes preparation time
plus chilling
213 Kcal per portion
14.7g fat per portion of which
7.9g is saturated
4 servings
Suitable for vegetarians

Green pepper 1

Ripe peaches 2

Cucumber ¼

Red onion 1 small

**Crisp lettuce such as
Cos or Romaine** 1

Greek-style black olives
75g (3oz)

Feta cheese 200g pack

Greek natural yogurt
6 tbsp

Lemon juice 3 tbsp

Mint sauce 1 tsp

Chopped mint 2 tbsp

**Salt and freshly ground
black pepper**

Cook's tip
•**Try replacing the
peaches with melon –
watermelon is especially
full of flavour.**

1 Halve and deseed the pepper. Cut into bite-sized chunks and place in a serving bowl. Cut the peaches in half and prise out the stone, then cut into thin slices and mix with the pepper.

2 Peel the cucumber, if preferred, and cut into small chunks. Peel the onion and cut into thin slices. Discard any damaged outer leaves from the lettuce. Wash and shake dry, then tear the leaves into small pieces and mix together in the serving bowl along with the olives.

3 Cut the feta cheese into cubes and toss into the salad. Cover and chill for at least an hour before serving.

4 Mix together the remaining ingredients and cover and chill until required. Serve the salad with the yogurt mixture as a dressing.

Root wedges with a herby dip

Root chips are popular all year round and here they make ideal dippers for a cheesy dip – perfect food for a buffet or party.

20 minutes preparation time plus standing
30 minutes cooking time
461 Kcal per portion
25.6g fat per portion of which
7.1g is saturated
4 servings
Suitable for vegetarians

Baking potatoes 2
Sweet potatoes 2
Parsnips 2
Carrots 2 large
Sunflower oil 2 tbsp
Coarsely ground black pepper
Garlic salt

For the dip:
Medium fat soft cheese with garlic and herbs 200g carton
Mayonnaise 4 tbsp
Low fat fromage frais 2 tbsp
Chopped chives 2 tbsp
Salt and freshly ground black pepper

1 Preheat the oven to 240°C/475°F/ Gas 9 and bring a large saucepan of lightly salted water to the boil.

2 Peel the potatoes and cut lengthwise into approximately 1cm (½in) wedges. Do the same with the sweet potatoes, parsnips and carrots. Add all the root wedges to the saucepan and cook for 5 minutes. Drain and set aside for 10 minutes to dry, then toss in the oil.

3 Line a baking sheet with baking parchment and place the wedges on top, spreading them out evenly. Sprinkle with black pepper and garlic salt to season. Bake the wedges in the oven for 20–25 minutes, turning occasionally, until golden brown all over. Drain on kitchen paper and keep warm.

4 Meanwhile, make the dip. Place the soft cheese in a bowl and carefully mix in the mayonnaise, fromage frais and chives. Season, cover and chill until required.

5 To serve, transfer the dip to a serving bowl and accompany with the root wedges to dip, plus other raw vegetable crudités, if liked.

Cook's tips
•**Experiment with other additions to the basic dip mix. Try fresh herbs, or lemon pulp and juice.**
•**For a lower fat option, serve with sweet chilli dipping sauce.**

Pesto roasted tomato tarts

It's worth making your own pesto sauce for this recipe, and it is very easy. The flavours are much more intense than ready-made varieties.

15 minutes preparation time
25 minutes cooking time
586 Kcal per portion
44.6g fat per portion of which
13.7g is saturated
4 servings
Suitable for vegetarians

Parmesan cheese 50g (2oz), freshly grated, plus extra shavings to serve

Garlic 1 clove, peeled and crushed

Basil a small bunch, plus a few extra leaves to garnish

Olive oil 4 tbsp

Pine nuts 50g (2oz)

Puff pastry 350g (12oz), thawed if frozen

Cherry vine tomatoes 350g (12oz)

1 Preheat the oven to 200°C/400°F/ Gas 6. Place the Parmesan, garlic, basil, olive oil and pine nuts in a blender and process until smooth.

2 Roll out the pastry on a lightly floured surface to form a 30cm (12in) square. Using a 15cm (6in) round pastry cutter or saucer, stamp out 4 circles and transfer to a lined baking sheet. Prick all over with a fork.

3 Divide the pesto sauce between the 4 circles and spread out evenly. Top each with a few cherry tomatoes, left whole, and bake in the oven for 20–25 minutes until lightly golden and puffed up. Serve each sprinkled with fresh basil leaves and extra shavings of fresh Parmesan.

If you haven't got a suitable blender, use a pestle and mortar to prepare the sauce. Start with the basil, garlic and pine nuts, then add the salt and cheese, pounding until the mixture is smooth.

Cook's tips
• **For a non-vegetarian version, add a few drained anchovy fillets.**
• **If preferred, arrange the toppings over ready-prepared mini bread pizza bases for a lower fat version.**
• **If you want to use ready-made pesto sauce, you'll need about 6 tbsp.**

Lancashire mushroom rolls

These crisp pastries make a substantial starter and are best baked just before serving for maximum crispness.

20 minutes preparation time
30 minutes cooking time
484 Kcal per portion
20.2g fat per portion of which
11.2g is saturated
4 servings
Suitable for vegetarians

Butter 40g (1½oz)

Onion 1, peeled and finely chopped

Garlic 2 cloves, peeled and crushed

Button mushrooms 110g (4oz), wiped and chopped

Fresh wholemeal breadcrumbs 75g (3oz)

Dried basil 1 tsp

Lancashire cheese 110g (4oz), crumbled

Salt and freshly ground black pepper

Filo pastry 8 sheets

1 Preheat the oven to 190°C/375°F/ Gas 5. Melt 15g (½oz) of the butter in a saucepan and add the onion and garlic. Sauté for 1 minute, then add the mushrooms and cook for a further 2 minutes.

2 Remove from the heat, stir in the breadcrumbs, basil and cheese and season to taste.

3 In a separate small saucepan, gently melt the remainder of the butter. Brush half of one sheet of pastry with the butter and fold in half lengthways. Place an eighth of the mixture onto the pastry, fold over the sides and roll up. Repeat with the remaining sheets.

4 Place on a greased baking sheet. Brush with melted butter and place in the oven. Bake for 20 minutes, until golden brown, and serve immediately with a green salad.

Cook's tip
•**Serve these pastries as a supper dish with vegetables, baby roast potatoes and a wholegrain mustard and mayonnaise dip.**

Smoked mackerel & dill pâté

This classic starter is always popular. Try accompanying it with a rhubarb or gooseberry compote for extra flavour.

15 minutes preparation time plus chilling
185 Kcal per portion
8.4g fat per portion of which
1.3g is saturated
4 servings
Suitable for freezing

Smoked mackerel 225g (8oz), skinned

Chopped dill 3 tbsp

Lemon juice 2 tbsp

Garlic 1 clove, peeled and crushed

Freshly ground black pepper

Double cream 150ml (¼ pint), lightly whipped

Egg 1, white only, whisked

Lemon wedges and chopped chives to garnish

Cook's tip
•**For added tang, stir in 1 tbsp each of finely chopped mini-gherkins and capers into the pâté mixture before chilling.**

1 Remove the skin from the back of the mackerel and place the flesh in a bowl. Add the dill, lemon juice, garlic and black pepper and mash together well or blend in a food processor. Fold in the cream and egg white.

2 Spoon the mixture onto individual plates and chill well.

3 Garnish the plates with lemon wedges and chives and serve with melba toast.

Lemony tuna lettuce cups

This recipe is quick and simple to prepare, yet it is an impressive and tasty way to serve canned tuna fish.

10 minutes preparation time plus chilling
220 Kcal per portion
12.1g fat per portion of which
2g is saturated
4 servings

Pink-skinned eating apple 1

Lemon 1, 2 tsp juice and 1 tsp finely grated zest

Celery 2 sticks

Seedless red grapes 110g (4oz)

Tuna in brine 2 x 185g cans, drained

Mayonnaise 4 tbsp

Freshly ground black pepper

Assorted small, crisp, lettuce leaves such as Little Gem, chicory or raddichio 24

Lemon wedges 4, to serve

1 Wash and pat dry the apple. Remove the core and then finely chop the apple, leaving the skin on. Place in a bowl and toss in the lemon juice.

2 Trim the celery and slice the stalks thinly, then mix with the apple. Cut the grapes in half and add to the bowl.

3 Add the tuna, mayonnaise and lemon zest, and mix together. Season with black pepper and cover and chill for at least 30 minutes.

4 When ready to serve, arrange six lettuce leaves on each serving plate. Pile the tuna mixture into each leaf and serve any remaining tuna mixture on the side. Sprinkle with extra black pepper if liked. Accompany with lemon wedges to squeeze over.

Cook's tips
•Replace the lemon with lime for a zestier flavour or use peeled prawns instead of tuna.
•For a lower fat version, use reduced fat mayonnaise and half low fat natural yogurt or fromage frais.

Smoked salmon & prawn salad

This delicate and pretty-looking salad would make an ideal starter to a romantic twilight dinner accompanied by some chilled pink champagne.

15 minutes preparation time
185 Kcal per portion
8.4g fat per portion of which
1.3g is saturated
4 servings

Cucumber ½

Strawberries 225g (8oz)

Smoked salmon 225g (8oz)

Peeled, cooked tiger prawns 110g (4oz)

Balsamic vinegar 2 tbsp

Olive oil 2 tbsp

Clear honey 1 tsp

Salt and freshly ground black pepper

Mint a small bunch, to garnish

Cook's tips

•**This salad's ingredients have delicate flavours, so it is best to serve it at room temperature or only slightly chilled.**
•**If preparing the salad in advance, removed it from the fridge for about 20 minutes before serving.**

1 Peel the cucumber, if preferred, and then halve lengthwise and thinly slice diagonally. Place in a mixing bowl.

2 Hull the strawberries. Halve them if large and add to the bowl with the cucumber. Toss the ingredients together gently and set aside.

3 Slice the smoked salmon into ribbon-like strips. Wash and pat dry the prawns. Whisk together the vinegar, oil and honey, and season.

4 To serve, pile the cucumber and strawberries on four serving plates and top each with some smoked salmon and prawns. Drizzle with dressing, sprinkle with ground black pepper, if liked, and top with a few mint leaves.

Cashew & vegetable stir-fry

This colourful dish is quick to prepare. The combination of crunchy veg and nuts works beautifully with the velvety texture of the cream and fromage frais.

10 minutes preparation time
10 minutes cooking time
337 Kcal per portion
25.8g fat per portion of which
8.8g is saturated
4 servings
Suitable for vegetarians

Butter 25g (1oz)

Garlic 2 cloves, peeled and crushed

Carrots 3, peeled and thinly sliced

Peppers 2, any colour, deseeded and sliced

Celery 4 sticks, sliced

Mushrooms 175g (6oz), wiped and sliced

Spring onions 8, sliced

Cashew nuts 110g (4oz), toasted

Chopped marjoram 2 tbsp

Double cream 3 tbsp

Fromage frais 4 tbsp

1 Melt the butter in a large frying pan or wok. Add the garlic and carrots and stir-fry for 3 minutes.

2 Add all the remaining vegetables and stir-fry for 1–2 minutes, stirring constantly.

3 Add the nuts, stir them in and transfer to a warm serving dish.

4 Add the marjoram and cream to the pan and heat until hot but not boiling. Remove from the heat and stir in the fromage frais.

5 Serve the stir-fried vegetables on a bed of rice or noodles with the sauce poured over the top.

Spice up this dish by frying grated fresh ginger with the garlic, plus, for a really hot mouthful, a chopped chilli. Adding lemon juice or soy sauce are other ideas for flavoursome variations on this vibrant recipe.

Cook's tip
•For a non-vegetarian version, replace the nuts with strips of cooked ham or chicken.

Tortilla

For an authentic taste of Spain, this dish is perfect served with a crisp salad, a handful of olives and some crusty bread.

20 minutes preparation time
1 hour 5 minutes cooking time plus cooling
248 Kcal per portion
10.5g fat per portion of which
2.4g is saturated
6 servings
Suitable for vegetarians

Potatoes 900g (2lb)
Olive oil 2 tbsp
Spanish onion 1, peeled and finely chopped
Garlic 2 cloves, peeled and finely chopped
Eggs 6 large
Salt and freshly ground black pepper
Chopped parsley 1 tbsp

Cook's tip

•**Alternatively, allow to cool completely, cut into wedges and chill for at least 2 hours. Serve cold. This makes great picnic food.**

1 Peel the potatoes and slice very thinly – the thinner you slice the potatoes, the quicker and more evenly they will cook.

2 Heat the oil in a large, deep frying pan and add the sliced potatoes, onion and garlic. Cook, turning frequently, over a medium heat for about 20 minutes until the potato begins to tenderise, but does not brown.

3 Beat together the eggs and plenty of seasoning and pour over the mixture. Keeping the heat low, cook the mixture until set, scraping the egg as it sets round the edge back into the middle – this will take about 30 minutes.

4 Slide onto a board and then invert back into the pan and continue to cook for a further 15 minutes until completely cooked through.

5 Remove from the heat and cool for 30 minutes. Cut into wedges and serve sprinkled with parsley.

Fresh pea & broad bean risotto

On a summer's evening, bring the flavour of Italy into your home with this Italian-style risotto. It's simple to make and cheaper than a trip abroad!

5 minutes preparation time
40 minutes cooking time
417 Kcal per portion
14.9g fat per portion of which
8.9g is saturated
6 servings
Suitable for freezing
Suitable for vegetarians

Shelled peas 175g (6oz), thawed if frozen

Shelled broad beans 175g (6oz), thawed if frozen

Vegetable stock 1.25 litres (2 pints)

Butter 50g (2oz)

Onion 1, peeled and finely chopped

Arborio risotto rice 400g (14oz)

Brie 150g (5oz)

Chopped tarragon 2 tbsp

Salt and freshly ground black pepper

1 Bring a small saucepan of water to the boil and cook the peas and beans for 4–5 minutes until just cooked. Drain and set aside, reserving the liquid to add to the stock.

2 Pour the stock into a saucepan and bring to the boil. Reduce the heat to a gentle simmer.

3 Meanwhile, melt the butter in a large saucepan and gently fry the onion for 2–3 minutes until softened but not browned. Add the rice and cook, stirring, for 2 minutes, until it has become well coated.

4 Add a ladleful of stock and cook gently, stirring, until it has been absorbed by the rice. Continue adding the stock to the rice ladle by ladle until half the stock is used and the rice is creamy.

5 Add the remaining stock until the risotto becomes thick, but not sticky. This will take about 25 minutes and should not be hurried. Just before serving, cut the Brie into bite-sized chunks. Then stir the peas, beans and tarragon into the rice, season and gently mix in the Brie. Serve immediately.

Cook's tip
•**Try other green vegetables like green beans, asparagus tips, sugar snap peas or broccoli florets. Add cubed pancetta for a non-vegetarian version.**

Griddled Halloumi cheese salad

**A simple yet substantial salad that looks impressive and tastes great.
It is best served as soon as the cheese is cooked.**

15 minutes preparation time
10 minutes cooking time
718 Kcal per portion
44.1g fat per portion of which
19g is saturated
4 servings
Suitable for vegetarians

**Crisp lettuce such as
Cos** ½ head

Cucumber ¼

Greek-style black olives
110g (4oz)

Red onion 1

Red wine vinegar 1 tbsp

Clear honey 2 tsp

Olive oil 2 tbsp

Pitta breads 4

Halloumi cheese 2 x
240g packs

**Ready-made honey and
mustard dressing** 4 tbsp
or follow recipe (step 4)
on page 60

1 Break up the lettuce, tear the leaves and place in a mixing bowl. Peel the cucumber, if preferred, and then cut into chunks and toss into the lettuce along with the olives and set aside.

2 Peel the onion and slice thinly, put in a bowl and add the vinegar and honey. Mix together. Heat 1 tbsp oil in a frying pan and add the onion mixture. Stir-fry for 6–7 minutes until golden and tender. Keep warm.

3 Preheat a ridged non-stick griddle pan or the grill to a hot setting and toast the pitta breads for 1–2 minutes on each side until crisp and golden. Keep warm.

4 Cut the cheese into slices about 1cm (½in) thick. Brush the frying griddle pan with a little oil and heat until very hot. Press a few slices of cheese at a time onto the pan for a few seconds until lightly golden. Turn over and fry again. Repeat with remaining cheese.

5 To serve, divide the salad between four serving plates. Arrange slices of warm cheese on top and cover with the caramelised onions. Serve sprinkled with the dressing, accompanied with the hot pitta bread.

This is an unusual warm salad that pleases so many of the senses – the aroma of the cooked cheese and onions, the range of textures and, of course, most important, the blend of flavours. What's more, it looks great – as you can see!

Cook's tip

•Halloumi cheese is a firm, white cheese with a rubbery texture and mild creamy taste. It is made with a mixture of cow's and sheep's milk, or all sheep's, and is often flavoured with mint. It stands up very well to cooking, and is perfect for grilling and frying.

Trout with almonds

A classic combination that makes the most of this subtly flavoured, popular oily fish; the cayenne adds a hint of spiciness.

15 minutes preparation time
10 minutes cooking time
530 Kcal per portion
32.5g fat per portion of which
12.6g is saturated
4 servings

Butter 75g (3oz)

Olive oil 2 tsp

Blanched almonds 50g (2oz)

Trout 4, gutted

Plain flour 4 tbsp

Salt and cayenne pepper

Lemon 1, cut into wedges, to garnish

1 Melt 25g (1oz) of the butter and all the oil in a large frying pan. Add the almonds and fry gently until golden brown. Turn off the heat and remove from the pan with a slotted spoon. Place the almonds in a heatproof dish, cover and keep warm.

2 Wash the trout and wipe dry with kitchen paper. Sprinkle the flour, salt and cayenne pepper together on a plate and then coat the trout, one by one, in the seasoned flour.

3 Reheat the frying pan (or use two pans to accommodate all 4 fish) and melt the remaining butter. Fry the trout for 4–5 minutes, turning once half-way through, until cooked through and golden.

4 Serve the fish with the hot butter and almonds, garnished with lemon wedges. Accompany the dish with new potatoes and peas.

Cook's tip
•**For a more indulgent dish, top the cooked trout with finely chopped, crispy, smoked bacon or pancetta.**

Salmon with cucumber sauce

Salmon and cucumber is a sophisticated yet simple blend of ingredients that will impress family and friends.

10 minutes preparation time
25 minutes cooking time
386 Kcal per portion
24.5g fat per portion of which
7.9g is saturated
4 servings

Salmon steaks 4 x 175g (6oz)

Lemon juice 4 tsp

Butter 15g (½oz)

Salt and freshly ground black pepper

Cucumber 1 large, peeled and deseeded

Dry white wine 125ml (4fl oz)

Soured cream 5 tbsp

Chopped dill 3 tbsp

Cook's tip
•**Take care not to overcook the cucumber otherwise the delicate flavour and texture will be lost.**

1 Preheat the oven to 170°C/325°F/ Gas 3. Place the salmon steaks on a large piece of lightly buttered foil on a baking sheet. Season lightly and sprinkle with lemon juice.

2 Wrap the foil loosely around the salmon, ensuring it is well sealed, and bake for 20–25 minutes until cooked. Leave in the foil.

3 Meanwhile, dice the cucumber finely. Melt the butter in a pan and sauté the cucumber for about 2 minutes until translucent.

4 Add the wine to the pan, bring to the boil and simmer for about 10 minutes until all the liquid has evaporated.

5 Remove from the heat, stir in the cream and dill and check the seasoning. Serve immediately with the warm fish accompanied by a creamy potato and chive mash and fresh green beans and peas.

Seafood & bacon kebabs

Wrapping delicate pieces of fish or shellfish in bacon before barbecuing is the ideal way to stop fish drying out over the fierce cooking heat.

30 minutes preparation time
4 minutes cooking time
265 Kcal per portion
16.3g fat per portion of which
5.3g is saturated
4 servings

Unsmoked back bacon
300g (11oz), trimmed

Raw king prawns 225g
(8oz), thawed if frozen

New Zealand mussels
400g (14oz), thawed if
frozen

**Salt and freshly ground
black pepper**

Courgettes 2

Lemon 1, plus lemon
wedges to serve

Olive oil 1 tbsp, if grilling

Chopped dill 1 tbsp, to
garnish

1 Slice each rasher of bacon lengthwise into thin strips about 1cm (½in) thick. Then cut each strip in half widthways.

2 Wash and pat dry the prawns, and place in a bowl. Remove the mussels from their shells and add to the prawns. Season with salt and pepper.

3 Trim the courgettes, cut into 1cm (½in) slices and then cut the slices in half. Cut the lemon into thin wedges.

4 Wrap a strip of bacon around each prawn and mussel and thread onto a kebab skewer along with pieces of courgette and lemon – you should have enough for eight skewers.

5 Place over hot coals and cook, turning frequently, for about 4 minutes, until cooked through and lightly golden.

6 Serve two skewers per person, on a bed of green salad leaves and coleslaw, sprinkled with dill and accompanied with lemon wedges to squeeze over.

Kebabs are so attractive, with their mix of colours and shapes. With recipes like this, it is often worth preparing a couple of meat-free kebabs too, for vegetarians.

Cook's tip
•**To cook indoors, preheat the grill or a ridged griddle to a medium/hot setting. Arrange the skewers on the grill rack, brush with oil and cook for 3–4 minutes on each side, until cooked through and golden. Drain on kitchen paper.**

Chicken with summer berries

A colourful and tasty combination of fruit and meat with a really summery feel. You can serve this hot, or cold as part of a salad.

15 minutes preparation time
30 minutes cooking time
221 Kcal per portion
6.7g fat per portion of which
1.6g is saturated
4 servings

Chicken breasts 4, skin left on

Salt and freshly ground black pepper

Sunflower oil 1 tbsp

Raspberries 110g (4oz), thawed if frozen

Blueberries 110g (4oz), thawed if frozen

Redcurrants 50g (2oz), thawed if frozen

Raspberry vinegar 4 tbsp

Clear honey 1 tbsp

Mint a few small leaves, to garnish

1 Wash and pat dry the chicken breasts and season on both sides.

2 Lightly brush a non-stick griddle pan or large frying pan with the oil and heat until hot. Press the chicken into the pan using a fish slice. Cook for 2 minutes then turn over and cook for a further 2 minutes to seal the chicken. Lower the heat to a low/medium setting and cook the chicken, turning frequently, for a further 20–25 minutes or until tender and cooked through.

3 Meanwhile, wash and pat dry the berries and currants, if using fresh, and set aside. Mix together the vinegar and honey, and season.

4 To serve, scatter a few berries and currants on four warm serving plates and top each with a chicken breast – remove the skin if preferred. Drizzle with the vinegar dressing and sprinkle with a few mint leaves. Serve with chunky chips (see Cook's Tips, page 40) and salad.

Griddled chicken served with a scattering of fruit looks so inviting. Try using grapes as an alternative. If the meat needs a little lift, sprinkle with some fresh lemon juice.

Cook's tip
•**Alternatively, allow the chicken to cool, chill and serve as a cold salad.**

Peanut chicken kebabs

This will be popular with children and adults alike and is perfect for an informal barbecue with friends. Serve with lots of different salads.

15 minutes preparation time plus marinating
20 minutes cooking time
224 Kcal per portion
16.1g fat per portion of which
4.8g is saturated
2 servings

For the marinade:

Crunchy peanut butter
2 tbsp

Soured cream
5 tbsp

Low fat fromage frais
150g (5oz)

Lemon juice 1 tbsp

Garlic 1 clove, peeled and crushed

Grated root ginger ½ tsp

Light soy sauce 1 tsp

Ground coriander 1 tsp

Tabasco sauce a few drops (optional)

Skinless chicken breasts
2

Cherry tomatoes 8

Red onion 1, peeled, quartered and split into pieces

Yellow pepper 1, deseeded and cut into pieces

Cook's tip
•**Try using pork or turkey, and consider other nut butters such as cashew or hazelnut, available from health food shops.**

1 Combine all the marinade ingredients thoroughly.

2 Cut the chicken into 2cm (¾in) cubes and place in a shallow dish. Spoon the marinade over the chicken and stir well. Cover and chill for 4–6 hours, stirring occasionally.

3 Thread the chicken, tomatoes, onion and pepper onto four skewers. Baste with the marinade and cook under a moderate grill or on a barbeque for 15–20 minutes, turning frequently and brushing with marinade, until thoroughly cooked. Serve with rice and salad.

Caribbean pork steaks

Pork is a rich meat and so complemented by fruit. Enjoy this dish outside in the garden, savouring the sounds and scents of summer.

15 minutes preparation time plus marinating
15 minutes cooking time
278 Kcal per portion
9.1g fat per portion of which
2.3g is saturated
4 servings

Lean boneless pork steaks or chops 4 x 150g (5oz) each
Salt and freshly ground black pepper
Dark muscovado sugar 1 tbsp
Dark rum 1 tbsp
Unsweetened pineapple juice 3 tbsp
Baby (Queen) pineapple 1
Red pepper 1 large
Sunflower oil 1 tbsp

1 Trim any excess fat from the pork, season on both sides and place in a shallow dish. Mix the brown sugar with the rum and pineapple juice and pour over the pork. Cover and chill for 30 minutes.

2 Meanwhile, peel the pineapple and cut into 1cm (½in) thick slices. Halve and deseed the pepper, cut into thick, flat wedges and set aside.

3 Brush a non-stick griddle or large frying pan with the oil and heat until hot. Drain the pork, reserving the juices, and press into the pan using a fish slice and cook on a high heat for 1 minute to seal. Turn over and cook for a further 1 minute. Lower the heat and continue to cook for 7–8 minutes, turning frequently, until golden, tender and cooked through. Drain.

4 Toss the pineapple and peppers in the reserved juices and cook the peppers in the pan for 2–3 minutes, until tender, and the pineapple for about 30 seconds on each side. Drain.

5 Serve the pork steaks on a bed of pineapple and peppers. Accompany with freshly cooked vegetables.

Cook's tips
•**Baby pineapples are particularly tender and sweet, but larger, ripe varieties work just as well. If you're using a larger pineapple, use half a medium-sized fruit, peel and slice, then cut the slices in half and remove the core before cooking.**
•**A pineapple should 'smell' sweet through its skin when ripe.**

Sticky sausages & roast veg

Even if you're vegetarian, you don't have to miss out on this tasty dish as there are many varieties of vegetarian sausage that would work very well instead.

5 minutes preparation time
30 minutes cooking time
361 Kcal per portion
26.7g fat per portion of which
7.9g is saturated
4 servings

Clear honey 2 tsp

Wholegrain mustard
2 tsp

Sweet chilli sauce 2 tsp,
plus extra to serve
(optional)

Thick pork sausages 8

Olive oil 2½ tbsp

Baby courgettes 200g
(7oz)

Baby leeks 200g (7oz)

Baby corn 200g (7oz)

**Cherry tomatoes on the
vine** 225g (8oz)

**Salt and freshly ground
black pepper**

Chopped chives 2 tbsp

1 Mix together the honey, mustard and chilli sauce and brush over the sausages. Lightly brush a non-stick griddle pan with a little oil and heat until hot, then press the sausages into the pan for 1 minute on each side to griddle mark. Reduce the heat and continue to cook the sausages, turning frequently, for a further 20 minutes until cooked through. Drain and keep warm.

2 Meanwhile, trim the courgettes and cut in half lengthwise. Trim and wash the leeks. Trim the baby sweetcorn.

3 Brush the same pan with a little more oil and reheat. Add the vegetables, pressing them into the pan for 1 minute. Then reduce the heat and continue to cook, stirring frequently, for about 5 minutes until the vegetables are lightly charred and just tender. Drain and keep warm.

4 Preheat the grill to a hot setting and arrange the tomatoes (still on the vine) on foil in the grill tray. Cook for 3–4 minutes until blistered and charred.

5 To serve, pile the vegetables onto warmed serving plates and top with the sausages. Season, sprinkle with chives and serve with extra chilli sauce, if liked.

Invite friends over for an impromptu barbecue
and treat them to this impressive yet easy dish.
Wash it down with a full and fruity red wine.

Cook's tip

•**To barbecue: place the sausages over white-hot coals and turn frequently, for about 10 minutes, until cooked through. Place the courgettes, leeks and corn in a vegetable basket or thread them on to skewers, turning them frequently – they will take 4–5 minutes to cook. The tomatoes will only take about a minute over hot coals.**

Mexican-style pasta

A light, delicately flavoured pasta dish with the spicy heat of chilli – add as much or as little as you like.

15 minutes preparation time
20 minutes cooking time
662 Kcal per portion
23.3g fat per portion of which
6.2g is saturated
4 servings

Penne or other pasta shapes 450g (1lb)

Lean, unsmoked, rindless back bacon 250g (9oz)

Dried chilli flakes ½–1 tsp

Spring onions 1 bunch

Avocados 2

Lime juice 1 tbsp

Salt and freshly ground black pepper

Coriander 15g pack, roughly chopped

Mature Cheddar 50g (2oz), grated

1 Bring a large saucepan of lightly salted water to the boil and cook the pasta according to the manufacturer's instructions – 10–12 minutes – until just tender. Drain well and return to the pan.

2 Meanwhile, cut the bacon into thin strips. Place the bacon and chilli, to taste, in a non-stick frying pan and cook, stirring frequently, for 6–7 minutes until crisp.

3 Trim the spring onions and slice thinly. Add to the bacon and chilli and stir-fry for a further minute. Stir this mixture into the drained pasta.

4 Just before serving, halve each avocado and remove the stone. Peel away the skin and slice thickly. Toss into the pasta mixture along with the lime juice and seasoning. Transfer to warmed serving bowls and serve, sprinkled with coriander and cheese.

Cook's tip
•**For a vegetarian version, replace the bacon with cooked and sliced vegetarian sausages.**

Sweet & spicy beef skewers

Here is an interesting and zesty way to enliven beef kebabs by adding fruity orange and the subtle spiciness of Worcestershire sauce.

20 minutes preparation time plus marinating
5 minutes cooking time
187 Kcal per portion
6g fat per portion of which
2.1g is saturated
4 servings

Worcestershire sauce 2 tbsp

Orange juice 1 tbsp, freshly squeezed

Sesame oil 1 tsp

Clear honey 1 tsp

Garlic 1 clove, peeled and crushed

Lean sirloin steak 450g (1lb), trimmed and very thinly sliced into ribbon-like shreds

Red pepper 1 small

Yellow pepper 1 small

Cook's tip
•**Alternatively, place under a hot grill for about 3–4 minutes on each side, until tender and cooked to your liking.**

1 Place eight bamboo skewers in a dish, cover with water, and set aside to soak. In a small bowl, mix together the Worcestershire sauce, orange juice, oil, honey and garlic. Place the steak in a shallow dish and gently turn it in the Worcestershire sauce mixture. Cover and chill in the refrigerator for at least an hour.

2 Meanwhile, halve and deseed the peppers and then cut them into even-sized chunks.

3 When ready to barbecue, drain the skewers and thread the pieces of steak on lengthwise – bending each piece to form an 'S' shape – along with chunks of pepper. Brush with any remaining marinade and cook, turning frequently, over hot coals for about 5 minutes or until done to your liking. Serve immediately with salad and rice.

White chocolate fondue

This is such a fun recipe to try, and the kids will love it too. It's also a sneaky way to get them to enjoy fruit!

15 minutes preparation time
5 minutes cooking time
351 Kcal per portion
27.6g fat per portion of which
10g is saturated
6 servings
Suitable for vegetarians

White chocolate 225g (8oz)

Double cream 200ml (7fl oz)

Orange 1, ½ tsp finely grated rind and 4 tbsp juice

To serve:

Skewers of cubed Jamaican ginger cake, slices of apple, orange, banana and strawberries, and marshmallows for dipping

Cook's tip
•**For a grown-up version, replace the orange juice with Cointreau or Grand Marnier, and use plain chocolate as an alternative.**

1 Break the chocolate into small pieces and place them in a fondue pot or small saucepan.

2 Add the cream, orange rind and juice, and heat very gently, stirring frequently, until the chocolate has melted and warmed through, and the texture is smooth and creamy.

3 Either serve straight from the fondue pot or pour into a heatproof bowl and serve with assorted 'dippers'.

Speedy summer berry sorbet

A super-quick way to enjoy a home-made sorbet. Simply make sure you have everything at hand before you begin, and serve straightaway.

10 minutes preparation time
119 Kcal per portion
1.6g fat per portion of which
0.9g is saturated
4 servings
Suitable for vegetarians

Assorted frozen small summer berries such as raspberries, blueberries, blackcurrants, redcurrants 500g (1lb 2oz)

Blackcurrant cordial 6 tbsp, undiluted

Mint leaves to decorate

Icing sugar to dust

1 Just before you are ready to serve this dessert, place the frozen fruits in a food processor or blender along with the blackcurrant cordial. Blend for a few seconds until well crushed and slightly slushy. You may have to blend the fruits a few times in order to crush them up.

2 Pile into serving glasses and decorate with mint. Dust lightly with icing sugar and serve immediately.

Cook's tip

• You can use you own assortment of fruit for this dessert; just make sure you choose small fruits like the berries and currants, and if you want to use larger soft fruits, such as strawberries, cut them into smaller pieces before freezing, so that they will crush in a blender more easily.

Pimms jellies

A jelly for grown-ups! Enjoy the flavours of summer with this fruity, soft-set cocktail. Serve with a cucumber and mint garnish for authenticity.

20 minutes preparation time plus setting
120 Kcal per portion
0.1g fat per portion of which
0g is saturated
4 servings

Powdered gelatine
1 sachet

Orange 1 large

Eating apple 1

Lemon 1, juice

Pimms 150ml (¼ pint)

Lemonade 450ml
(16fl oz), chilled

Lemon and cucumber slices and mint sprigs to decorate

1 Pour 4 tbsp boiling water into a bowl and sprinkle in the gelatine. Stir until dissolved, then set aside.

2 Slice off the top and bottom of the orange. Using a small, sharp knife, slice off the skin, taking away as much of the pith as possible. Holding the orange over a bowl, slice in between each segment to release the flesh and juice into the bowl.

3 Core and finely chop the apple and toss in the lemon juice to prevent browning. Mix into the orange segments. Divide between four serving glasses or tumblers.

4 Mix the Pimms with the gelatine and lemonade and pour over the fruit. Chill for 1–2 hours until set. Serve decorated with slices of lemon and cucumber and sprigs of mint.

Dressing the jelly with mint sprigs, cucumber and fruit is a lovely finishing touch that makes this dessert that little bit special. Garnish just before serving.

Cook's tips
•If the gelatine does not thoroughly dissolve because the liquid has cooled too soon, complete the process by standing the bowl in a pan of warm water over a low heat. Stir well. Never allow the gelatine mixture to boil.
•For a healthier version, use low calorie or diet lemonade.

Green tea fruit salad

An attractive combination of colours and flavours makes this dessert the perfect ending for a dinner party, although it is simple enough to make everyday, too.

20 minutes preparation time plus chilling
74 Kcal per portion
0.3g fat per portion of which
0g is saturated
4 servings
Suitable for vegetarians

Japanese green tea bag 1

Kiwi fruit 2

Lychees 225g (8oz)

Green-fleshed melon such as Galia ¼

Seedless green grapes 110g (4oz)

Lime 1

Dry sherry 2 tbsp (optional)

Caster sugar to taste

1 Place the tea bag in a small heatproof jug and pour over 150ml (¼ pint) boiling water. Leave to infuse for 5 minutes then discard the bag and allow the tea to cool. Cover and chill for 30 minutes.

2 Peel and thinly slice the kiwi fruit and peel, halve and stone the lychees. Remove the seeds from the melon and slice off the skin. Cut the flesh into small pieces. Separate the grapes from their stalks. Put all the fruits into a bowl, cover and chill until required.

3 Meanwhile, finely grate the rind from the lime and extract the juice.

4 Once the tea has cooled, mix in the sherry, if using, lime rind (reserving some to decorate) and juice and add sufficient sugar to taste.

5 To serve, arrange the fruits in four serving bowls and drizzle over the tea mixture. Decorate with the reserved lime rind and serve.

Cook's tip
•If fresh lychees are unavailable, look out for them in cans. You will need to drain them well and rinse off the syrup. Otherwise, replace the lychees with chunks of fresh pineapple.

Gooseberry & almond tart

Just coming into season in early summer, gooseberries make great pies, crumbles and tarts.

15 minutes preparation time
35 minutes cooking time
427 Kcal per portion
28.1g fat per portion of which
9.1g is saturated
8 servings
Suitable for freezing
Suitable for vegetarians

Dessert shortcrust pastry 375g pack, thawed if frozen

Butter 50g (2oz)

Caster sugar 110g (4oz)

Ground almonds 100g pack

Eggs 1 whole and 1 egg yolk

Brandy 1 tbsp

Gooseberries 250g (9oz)

Crème fraîche or double cream to serve

Cook's tips

•**If you have lots of gooseberries, bag them in 500g (1lb 2oz) quantities. They freeze very well. Thaw them in a sieve over a bowl.**

•**Cooking the tart on the second shelf from the bottom of the oven should help the pastry to cook, which means that you then won't get a soggy-bottomed tart.**

1 On a lightly floured surface, roll out the pastry fairly thinly to line a 23cm (9in) fluted loose-based flan tin, ensuring there is about 3mm (⅛in) pastry above the flan rim after trimming. You will have pastry left over to make some jam tarts.

2 Preheat the oven to 200°C/400°F/ Gas 6. Chill the pastry case while the oven heats up, or longer if you have the time.

3 Melt the butter in a large bowl (in the microwave or over a pan of simmering water). Add all but 1 tbsp of the sugar and beat well. Stir in the ground almonds, egg and egg yolk and brandy. Spoon the mixture into the flan case.

4 Put the gooseberries on top and sprinkle with the remaining sugar. Bake in the bottom half of the oven for 30–35 minutes until firm and golden brown. Serve warm or at room temperature with crème fraîche or double cream.

Tart au citron with cassis sauce

A classic summer dessert, bursting with citrus tanginess. If you have fresh blackcurrants, then lightly stew them in the cordial and sweeten to taste.

30 minutes preparation time plus chilling
40 minutes cooking time
442 Kcal per portion
22.8g fat per portion of which
12.4g is saturated
6 servings
Suitable for freezing
Suitable for vegetarians

For the pastry:
Plain flour 150g (5oz)
Caster sugar 50g (2oz)
Unsalted butter 75g (3oz)
Egg yolks 2
Vanilla essence 1 tsp

For the filling:
Lemons 3 small
Caster sugar 110g (4oz)
Unsalted butter 50g (2oz), melted
Eggs 4

For the sauce:
Blackcurrants in natural juice 290g can
Blackcurrant cordial 2 tbsp, undiluted

Icing sugar for dusting
Crème fraîche to serve

Cook's tips
•**For an alternative flavour, replace the lemons with four limes.**
•**To speed up the preparation, use bought dessert shortcrust pastry, as on page 93.**

1 First make the pastry. Sieve the flour into a bowl and add the sugar. Rub in the butter until the mixture resembles large breadcrumbs. Continuing to use your fingertips, mix in the egg yolks and vanilla essence and bring the mixture together to form a dough.

2 Press the mixture into a greased 23cm (9in) fluted loose-bottomed flan tin that is 2.5cm (1in) deep, and lightly prick all over with a fork. Preheat the oven to 200°C/400°F/Gas 6. Place the lined flan tin in the freezer for 15 minutes until very firm.

3 Bake on a rigid baking sheet for 12–15 minutes until lightly golden. Remove the pastry case from the oven and reduce the oven temperature to 180°C/350°F/Gas 4.

4 Meanwhile, make the filling. Scrub the lemons and then finely grate the rind. Extract the juice and strain into a bowl. Mix in the lemon rind, sugar and melted butter. Beat the eggs together and strain through a sieve into the lemon mixture. Stir well.

5 Pour the filling into the pastry case and bake in the oven for about 25 minutes until just set. Allow to cool in the tin and then remove and chill for at least 2 hours.

6 For the sauce, press the blackcurrants with the canning juice through a nylon sieve to remove the skins, and then mix the purée with the cordial. Cover and chill in the refrigerator until required.

7 To serve, slice the tart into equal wedges, lightly dust with icing sugar and serve with the cassis sauce and crème fraîche.

The drizzled sauce gives a great lift to this dish, especially when the tart is sprinkled with a dusting of icing sugar.

Strawberry shortcakes

The very essence of an English summer presented on a plate. Melt-in-the-mouth shortcake with whipped cream and sweet strawberries – bliss.

20 minutes preparation time plus chilling and cooling
20 minutes cooking time
472 Kcal per portion
33.4g fat per portion of which
19.4g is saturated
10 shortcakes
Shortcake biscuits suitable for freezing
Suitable for vegetarians

Unsalted butter 225g (8oz), softened

Caster sugar 110g (4oz)

Plain flour 300g (11oz)

Salt a pinch

Ground almonds 50g (2oz)

Small strawberries 225g (8oz)

Whipping cream 300ml (½ pint)

Strawberry jam 2 tbsp soft-set

Caster sugar for dusting

1 First make the shortcakes. Cream together the butter and sugar until light and fluffy, then mix in the flour, salt and ground almonds until the mixture clings together to form a dough. Turn onto a floured surface and knead gently until smooth.

2 Lightly press and roll the dough to flatten it to a thickness of 6mm (¼in) and, using a 7.5cm (3in) round cutter, stamp out as many shapes as you can. Re-roll the dough and continue stamping out shapes until all the dough is used up. You should end up with about 20 circles.

3 Line a baking sheet with baking parchment and place the shortcake circles on the sheet. Prick with a fork and chill for 40 minutes.

4 Preheat the oven to 180°C/350°F/ Gas 4 and bake the shortcake biscuits for 15–20 minutes until lightly golden. Set aside to cool.

5 To finish, wash the strawberries and hull and slice them. Whisk the cream into soft peaks, and then spoon onto half the shortcake biscuits. Top with a few strawberry slices and a drizzle of jam. Add a small dollop of cream and then sandwich a plain shortcake on top. Dust very lightly with sugar and serve immediately.

Cook's tip

•Use different fruits such as raspberries, blueberries or cherries, and use the same-flavour jam. For a romantic supper-time dessert, cut heart-shaped shortcakes.

Rich poppy seed & almond cake

Here is a sweet and sticky, rich cake oozing with flavour. Serve lightly chilled with fresh fruit and plenty of cream.

20 minutes preparation time
50 minutes cooking time plus chilling
501 Kcal per slice
33.1g fat per slice of which
4.2g is saturated
8 slices
Cake suitable for freezing without orange topping
Suitable for vegetarians

Light olive oil 175ml (6fl oz)

Unbleached caster sugar 250g (9oz)

Eggs 2 large

Ground almonds 150g (5oz)

Oranges 3 large, 1 tsp finely grated rind and 4 tbsp freshly squeezed juice from 1 orange

Dry polenta 75g (3oz)

Poppy seeds 15g (½oz)

Baking powder ½ tsp

Vanilla essence ½ tsp

Crème fraîche for serving

1 Preheat the oven to 180°C/350°F/ Gas 4. Line the base of an 18cm (7in) spring-release cake tin with baking parchment. Lightly grease the sides.

2 Whisk together the olive oil, 175g (6oz) of the caster sugar and eggs and then fold in the ground almonds, orange rind, polenta, poppy seeds, baking powder and vanilla essence.

3 Spoon the mixture into the prepared tin and bake for about 50 minutes or until a skewer inserted into the centre comes out clean.

4 While the cake is baking, make the syrup. Place the remaining sugar in a small saucepan with the orange juice and heat gently until the sugar dissolves. Bring to the boil and cook for 3–4 minutes until syrupy. Set aside.

5 Meanwhile, using a sharp knife, slice the top and bottom off the oranges and cut off the peel, taking away as much of the pith as possible. Cut the oranges into thin slices and place in a shallow bowl. Set aside.

6 Loosen the cake from the tin by running a knife around the edge. Skewer the cake all over while still warm and drizzle over the syrup. Allow to cool, then release from the tin. Place on a serving plate and chill for 1 hour. Serve with crème fraîche and the fresh orange segments.

Cook's tip
•**Flavour this cake with lemon or lime instead of orange, and serve with Greek natural yogurt, honey and fresh figs.**

Autumn

Spanish tomato soup

As the leaves fall from the trees, we turn to warming, comfort food. This soup – vibrant in both taste and colour – offers just this.

15 minutes preparation time
40 minutes cooking time
150 Kcal per portion
9g fat per portion of which
5.3g is saturated
6 servings
Suitable for freezing (add cream and mint garnish when reheating)
Suitable for vegetarians

Butter 25g (1oz)

Onions 2, peeled and sliced

Tomatoes 900g (2lb), roughly chopped

Sweet paprika ½ tsp

Dry sherry 6 tbsp

Sugar 1 tbsp

Salt 1 tsp

Mint leaves 4 tbsp finely shredded, plus leaves to garnish

Vegetable stock 400ml (14fl oz), plus extra for thinning soup (optional)

Whipping cream 5 tbsp, lightly whipped

Cook's tip

•**If you have a glut of homegrown tomatoes, freeze some for use during the winter as they are perfect for making tomato sauce (see page 127) and soups.**

1 Melt the butter in a large, lidded saucepan. Add the onions and cook them gently until soft but not brown.

2 Add the tomatoes to the onions with the paprika, sherry, sugar, salt, mint and stock. Stir well, cover and simmer for 30 minutes, stirring occasionally.

3 Cool slightly and then purée in a blender or food processor until smooth, in batches if necessary. Pour the soup through a sieve back into the saucepan. Add extra stock to give the desired consistency and reheat. Serve hot, swirled with whipped cream and garnished with mint leaves.

Mixed vegetable soup

This is a chunky and substantial vegetable soup, ideal for a mid-week meal or Saturday lunch following an autumnal stroll.

40 minutes preparation time
45 minutes–1 hour cooking time
169 Kcal per portion
8.7g fat per portion of which
3.7g is saturated
8 servings
Suitable for freezing
Suitable for vegetarians if using vegetable stock

Butter 50g (2oz)

Olive oil 2 tbsp

Onion 1 very large, peeled and chopped

Carrots 350g (12oz), peeled and cut into small dice

Parsnips 225g (8oz), peeled and cut into small dice

Potatoes 350g (12oz), peeled and cut into small dice

Swede 350g (12oz), peeled and cut into small dice

Tomatoes 400g can

Mixed dried herbs 2 tsp

Vegetable or chicken stock 1 litre (1¾ pints)

Salt and freshly ground black pepper

Snipped chives to garnish

1 Heat the butter and oil together in a very large, lidded saucepan until the butter melts, then add the onion and cook gently, without browning, until slightly softened.

2 Add all the remaining vegetables to the saucepan, stir well and cook gently for 4–5 minutes, again without letting them brown.

3 Add the canned tomatoes and their juice, the herbs and chosen stock to the pan. Bring to the boil, then reduce the heat, cover and cook gently for 45 minutes–1 hour, until the vegetables are tender but not cooked so much that they are broken up.

4 Season soup to taste and serve hot sprinkled with chives.

Cook's tip
•For freezing, allow the soup to cool, then pour (in desired quantities) into clean containers, cover and freeze. It can be kept for up to 3 months.

Pumpkin soup

Pumpkin soup is a traditional favourite for Bonfire Night, particularly when served in mugs – ideal for warming cold hands!

10 minutes preparation time
40 minutes cooking time
183 Kcal per portion
8.8g fat per portion of which
5.4g is saturated
4 servings
Suitable for freezing
Suitable for vegetarians

Butter 25g (1oz)

Onion 1, peeled and chopped

Carrot 1, peeled and chopped

Peeled pumpkin 350g (12oz), roughly chopped

Milk 750ml (1¼ pints)

Salt and freshly ground black pepper

Natural yogurt 150g (5oz)

Dried pumpkin seeds to garnish (optional)

1 Melt the butter in a large, lidded saucepan and add the onion and carrot. Cook gently for about 5 minutes until the onions are soft but not brown.

2 Add the pumpkin, milk and seasoning and bring gently to the boil, then reduce the heat, cover and simmer for 30 minutes, until all the vegetables are soft.

3 Transfer soup to a blender or food processor and purée until smooth, in batches if necessary. Return to the saucepan, reheat gently and serve swirled with yogurt and garnished with pumpkin seeds. Accompany with hunks of warmed bread.

If you have been busy making pumpkin lanterns for Halloween, you will have plenty of spare pumpkin flesh. This soup is the perfect solution, and tastes delicious too!

Cook's tips

• Many varieties of squash are available all year round, but pumpkins are only with us for a short while – so it's worth steaming the flesh, puréeing and then freezing it for use throughout the year, to make pumpkin pie and cheesecakes as well as for adding to stews and casseroles.
• If pumpkin is not available, try the recipe with butternut squash instead, or use canned pumpkin purée.

Autumn celery soup

This pretty soup is special enough to serve as a dinner party starter but at the same time is very inexpensive to make.

20 minutes preparation time
30 minutes cooking time
159 Kcal per portion
13.6g fat per portion of which
8.3g is saturated
4–6 servings
Suitable for freezing without cream
Suitable for vegetarians

Butter 50g (2oz)

Onion 1 large, peeled and chopped

Celery 1 whole head, approximately 500g (1lb 2oz)

Vegetable stock 1.25 litres (2 pints)

Salt and freshly ground black pepper

Single cream 4–6 tbsp

Sliced celery and snipped chives to garnish

Crusty bread, Stilton and crisp Cox's apples to accompany

1 Melt the butter in a large, lidded saucepan, add the onion and cook until translucent and slightly softened, taking care not to let it brown.

2 Add the celery and stock to the saucepan and bring to the boil, then reduce the heat, cover and cook gently for 25–30 minutes, or until the celery and onions are very soft. Remove the soup from the heat and leave to cool a little. Then purée in a blender or food processor until smooth, in batches if necessary.

3 Pour the soup through a sieve back into the saucepan and reheat, seasoning to taste. Stir in the cream and heat for 1–2 minutes, but do not allow the soup to boil.

4 Serve in individual bowls, sprinkled with celery and chives, and accompany with crusty bread and Stilton, and apples.

Cook's tips
•**For the very best flavour, look out for British celery, untrimmed and with the leaves attached. It will take longer to trim and scrub, but it is worth the effort.**
•**For the best flavour, serve Stilton and apples at room temperature.**

Red cabbage salad

This crisp, red cabbage salad can be served as a starter, or as an accompaniment to either hot or cold meats, fish and poultry.

20 minutes preparation time plus marinating
329 Kcal per portion
24.9g fat per portion of which
3g is saturated
4–6 servings
Suitable for vegetarians

Red cabbage 450g (1lb), white woody core removed

Spring onions 6, trimmed

Seedless raisins 50g (2oz)

Unsalted cashew nuts 110g (4oz), lightly toasted

For the dressing:
Wholegrain mustard 1 tsp

Caster sugar 1 tsp

Rice wine vinegar 2 tbsp

Extra-virgin olive oil 4–5 tbsp

Garlic 2 cloves, peeled and crushed

Chopped flat-leaved parsley 6 tbsp

Cook's tip
•**This salad can also be made with finely shredded white cabbage or Savoy cabbage, or a mixture of all three!**

1 Very finely shred the cabbage – by hand with a large sharp knife, or using a food processor. Then place in a large bowl.

2 Cut the spring onions in half lengthways and then cut each piece in half widthways (or, into three if onions are very large). Cut each piece into very fine shreds lengthways and add to the cabbage, along with the raisins and cashew nuts.

3 In a small bowl, whisk together all the dressing ingredients, except for 2 tbsp of the parsley. Pour the dressing over the salad and mix well. Cover and leave to stand for at least 30 minutes before serving.

4 Transfer the salad to a serving bowl and scatter with the remaining parsley just before serving.

English garden ratatouille

If you are lucky enough to have a veg patch, enjoy the fruits of your labour really simply in this ratatouille. If not, try buying organic for better flavour.

25 minutes preparation time
45 minutes–1 hour cooking time
222 Kcal per portion
17.4g fat per portion of which
2.5g is saturated
4–6 servings
Suitable for vegetarians

Olive oil 6 tbsp

Onions 2 red, peeled, halved and thickly sliced lengthways

Carrots 225g (8oz), peeled and sliced

Tomatoes 350g (12oz), skinned (see Cook's Tip, page 158), deseeded and roughly chopped

Small courgettes 300g (11oz), trimmed and sliced

Garlic 4–6 cloves, peeled

Bouquet garni made with medium–large sprig of parsley, small sprig of fresh thyme and 1 bay leaf, tied with string

Chopped flat-leaved parsley 4 tbsp

Salt and freshly ground black pepper

1 In a heavy-based, lidded saucepan, heat 4 tbsp of the oil, add the onions and carrots and cook over a moderate heat for 10 minutes, or until slightly softened – but do not allow to brown.

2 Add the tomatoes to the saucepan and cook for 3–4 minutes, then add the courgettes, garlic and bouquet garni. Cover the surface of the vegetables closely with non-stick baking paper, then cover with a lid and cook gently for 45 minutes– 1 hour until the vegetables are softened, but not broken up.

3 Place a sieve or colander over a bowl and carefully pour the cooked vegetables into it, to drain.

4 Pour the vegetable juices back into the saucepan, bring to the boil and cook for 2–3 minutes, until reduced and slightly thickened. Then return the vegetables to the saucepan, add the remaining oil and the chopped parsley, season and mix gently.

5 Serve the ratatouille hot, as an accompaniment to cooked chicken,or grilled fish or meat steaks. Alternatively, cool and then chill – and serve as a starter, accompanied with warm, crusty French bread.

Indulge in good, old-fashioned British produce. This English version of a Mediterranean classic is scrumptious indeed.

Cook's tips
•Take care not to overcook the vegetables; they should be softened but still retain their shape.
•Covering the surface closely with greaseproof paper prevents excess evaporation of the vegetables' juices.

Tomatoes in a spicy dressing

Set your taste buds tingling with this unusual salad. It is the perfect accompaniment to poached fish, particularly trout or salmon.

20 minutes preparation time
225 Kcal per portion
17.5g fat per portion of which
2.5g is saturated
4 servings
Suitable for vegetarians

Large, ripe tomatoes
680g (1½lb), cored (see Cook's Tip)

Onion 1 medium–large, peeled

Pickled gherkins 3–4

Chopped parsley
4–5 tbsp

For the dressing:
Olive oil 6 tbsp

Rice vinegar 3 tbsp

Coarsely ground black pepper ½ tsp

Chilli powder ½ tsp

Ground coriander ½ tsp

Caster sugar ½ tsp

Salt ¼–½ tsp

Cook's tip
•**For the very best flavour, always bring tomatoes to room temperature before using. To remove the centre core, insert the tip of a small pointed knife to one side of the core, then cut around it at an angle, enabling it to be removed in one, cone-shaped piece, retaining the seeds.**

1 Cut the tomatoes and onions into thin slices widthways. Separate the onion slices into rings. Cut the gherkins into thin slices lengthways, then into long, thin strips.

2 Arrange half of the tomato slices in the bottom of a shallow serving dish, then scatter half the onion rings over the top. Add half of the gherkins and sprinkle with half of the parsley. Repeat with all of the remaining ingredients, filling the dish.

3 To make the dressing, place all the ingredients in a small saucepan. Gently heat and whisk together until hot, but not boiling. Pour over the layered salad and leave to stand for 5–10 minutes before serving.

Marinated pilchards on toast

As the temperature falls, this **Mediterranean-influenced dish** will warm you through with memories of sunny climates.

20 minutes preparation time
10 minutes cooking time
417 Kcal per portion
27g fat per portion of which
4.4g is saturated
4 servings as a snack, 2 as a supper dish

Large fresh sardines or fresh pilchards 4, approximately 110g (4oz) each, heads removed, gutted, de-scaled, washed and dried

Olive oil 6 tbsp

Mixed dried herbs 1½ tsp

Tomato purée 1 tbsp

Cayenne pepper or hot chilli powder ⅛–¼ tsp

Garlic 1 large clove, peeled and crushed

Mediterranean-style ciabatta bread 4 slices, 1cm (½in) thick, cut diagonally to the same length as the prepared fish

Basil leaves 4 large or 8 small

Coarsely ground black pepper

1 Make two light, diagonal cuts through the skin on both sides of each fish.

2 On a deep plate, mix together 2 tbsp of the oil with the dried herbs, tomato purée and cayenne or hot chilli powder. Add the pilchards or sardines and turn in the mixture until evenly coated. Cover and leave to stand for at least 10 minutes.

3 Meanwhile, preheat the grill to high. Mix the remaining oil with the garlic and brush over both sides of the bread.

4 Place the bread on a rack in the grill pan and lightly toast, one side only, under the grill. Remove from the grill and turn over the bread.

5 Place the basil leaves inside each marinated fish, and then place on the untoasted sides of the bread and grill for approximately 2 minutes until they begin to brown and are cooked through on that side. Then turn over the fish and cook on the other side – during cooking their delicious juices will be absorbed by the bread.

6 Sprinkle with black pepper and serve immediately while still hot.

Cook's tip

•**To prevent the bread from over-browning, do not place the grill pan too near the heating element while cooking the fish.**

Filo cases with prawns

Seafood and filo pastry is always a winning combination of flavours and textures. It makes an impressive starter when entertaining friends.

30 minutes preparation time
15 minutes cooking time
482 Kcal per portion
20.1g fat per portion of which
8.2g is saturated
4 servings

Filo pastry 8 x 15cm (6in) squares
Olive oil for brushing
Butter 50g (2oz)
Garlic 1–2 cloves, peeled and crushed
Chopped parsley 4–5 tbsp
Large peeled prawns 200g (7oz), thawed and drained if frozen
Smoked trout fillet 125g pack, flaked and boned (if necessary)
Freshly ground black pepper
Lemon 1, cut into wedges to garnish and for squeezing
Watercress to garnish

1 Preheat the oven to 180°C/350°F/Gas 4. Place four ovenproof mugs (preferably tall and thin, rather than short and wide) upside-down on a baking tray, spaced well apart. Place a 15cm (6in) square of non-stick baking paper over each mug. Mould the paper firmly over the top and down the side.

2 Take one of the filo squares, brush it lightly with oil and drape it loosely, oiled side down, over one of the mugs. Brush another square of pastry and drape it at a 45-degree angle to the first one, to resemble a water lily.

3 Make three more cases in the same way, and then bake for 7–8 minutes, until golden, but not over-browned. Leave to cool, then carefully remove the cases from the mugs and store in an airtight tin until ready to use.

4 Place the filo cases on individual plates. Heat the butter in a frying pan until melted, then add the garlic, parsley and prawns and heat gently until the prawns are hot. Don't overheat, as the prawns will toughen.

5 Carefully mix in the smoked trout and season lightly with black pepper only, as prawns tend to be salty. Carefully spoon into the filo cases, garnish with lemon wedges and watercress and serve immediately.

Cook's tip
•Prawns are so convenient to buy frozen. When defrosting them, rinse under cold running water to get rid of any brine, then revitalise by soaking the prawns in a little lemon juice.

Clever use of filo pastry turns this dish into something really special. Don't add the filling until the last moment, to prevent the pastry soaking up sauce and becoming soggy.

Cauliflower gratin

This wholesome gratin is quick to make and extremely satisfying so it is perfect for a weekday dinner.

15 minutes preparation time
30 minutes cooking time
420 Kcal per portion (as a main meal)
21.7g fat per portion of which **11.3g** is saturated
4 servings as an accompaniment, or 2 as a supper dish
Suitable for vegetarians

Cauliflower 1 medium–large, trimmed and cut into florets

Butter 40g (1½oz)

Onion 1 large, peeled and sliced

Mushrooms 110g (4oz), wiped and halved

Eggs 2 large, hard boiled, shelled and roughly chopped

Plain flour 25g (1oz)

Milk 300ml (½ pint)

Double Gloucester cheese 75g (3oz), grated

Sweetcorn kernels 175g (6oz), canned or frozen, well drained

Natural yogurt 150g (5oz)

Fresh breadcrumbs 25g (1oz)

1 Bring a saucepan of salted water to the boil, add the cauliflower and cook for 5 minutes, or until only just tender.

2 Meanwhile, melt 15g (½oz) of the butter in a saucepan and cook the onion and mushrooms for 5 minutes.

3 Drain the cooked cauliflower and place in a flameproof dish with the onions and mushrooms and add the chopped eggs.

4 Melt the remaining butter in a saucepan and stir in the flour. Add the milk and bring to the boil, stirring until smooth. Add half of the cheese and stir until melted. Remove from the heat and stir in the yogurt and sweetcorn.

5 Pour the sauce evenly over the vegetables. Mix the remaining cheese with the breadcrumbs and sprinkle over the sauce.

6 Heat the grill to moderate. Place the cauliflower gratin under the grill and cook until golden brown and bubbling hot, reducing the heat if necessary to prevent cheese and breadcrumbs burning. Serve immediately with roast meat or crusty bread and salad.

Cook's tip
•**Put the cauliflower florets upright in the saucepan, then just cover the stalks in water. That way the tops won't overcook.**

Leeks in a triple cheese sauce

Enjoy local British cheeses at their best – in a wonderfully rich sauce, served simply with leek and tomatoes.

45 minutes preparation time
30 minutes cooking time
296 Kcal per portion (as an accompaniment)
17.3g fat per portion of which
10.3g is saturated
4 servings as an accompaniment, 2 as a supper dish
Suitable for vegetarians

Leeks 400g (14oz), approximately 4, evenly sized, ready trimmed, washed and dried

Vegetable stock 300ml (½ pint), preferably unsalted

Milk for making stock up to 300ml (½ pint) after cooking leeks

Butter 25g (1oz)

Plain flour 25g (1oz)

Mature Cheddar cheese 40g (1½oz), grated

Double Gloucester cheese 40g (1½oz), grated

Cheshire cheese 40g (1½oz), grated

Freshly ground black pepper

Fresh white breadcrumbs 4 tbsp

Tomatoes 2, core removed (see Cook's Tip, page 108) and cut into wedges

Cook's tip
• **If preferred, just one or two cheeses may be used, depending on what is available. Use a total weight of 125g (4½oz).**

1 Cut each leek into 3 evenly sized pieces and place in a single layer in a shallow, lidded saucepan. Add the stock, cover and bring to the boil. Reduce the heat and cook gently for 10–15 minutes or until softened, taking care not to overcook.

2 Drain the stock from the leeks into a measuring jug and make up to 300ml (½ pint) with milk. Dry the leeks well on kitchen paper and place in a single layer in a shallow, ovenproof dish. Preheat the oven to 220°C/ 425°F/Gas 7.

3 Melt the butter in a saucepan, stir in the flour and add the stock. Bring to the boil, stirring continuously. Add three-quarters of each cheese and stir until melted. Season with black pepper only, as the cheeses are salty.

4 Pour the sauce evenly over the leeks. Arrange the tomato wedges on top. Mix all of the remaining grated cheese with the breadcrumbs and sprinkle evenly over the sauce.

5 Bake in the centre of the oven for approximately 30 minutes, or until golden brown and bubbling hot. Serve immediately with grilled chicken or fish.

Haddock in lemon butter sauce

When you next fancy haddock for dinner, don't be tempted to dash to the chip shop. Try this recipe; it's easy to make and much more healthy!

5 minutes preparation time
15 minutes cooking time
274 Kcal per portion
7.6g fat per portion of which
4.3g is saturated
4 servings

Haddock fillet 800g (1¾lb), skinned and any bones removed, if necessary

Milk 300ml (½ pint)

Lemon 1, finely grated rind and juice (optional), plus extra rind to garnish

Salt and freshly ground black pepper

Cornflour 2 tbsp

Butter 25g (1oz), cubed

Chopped flat-leaved parsley to garnish

1 Cut the haddock into 4 portions. Place in a large, lidded frying pan (or two, if necessary) in a single layer, add the milk and lemon rind (dividing between two pans, if necessary), and season well.

2 Bring the milk to the boil, then reduce the heat, cover and simmer gently for 4–5 minutes, or until the haddock turns opaque and only just starts to flake easily, taking care not to overcook as the portions will break up.

3 With a large fish slice, carefully lift each piece of haddock from the pan(s), allowing the excess liquid to drain off, and place on a large serving dish. Cover and keep warm while making the sauce.

4 Blend the cornflour with 2 tbsp of cold water, then stir into the poaching liquid and bring back to the boil, stirring continuously, until thickened. Whisk in the butter and season to taste, if necessary – adding a little lemon juice if wished.

5 Place the haddock on serving plates and spoon over the sauce. Garnish with lemon rind and chopped parsley and serve, accompanied with green beans, baby carrots and potatoes.

Try other varieties of meaty, white fish, such as hake, cod and whiting. These have the firm flesh needed for this dish, but you may need to adjust the cooking times a little to avoid overcooking.

Cook's tip
•**For a thicker, creamier sauce, stir crème fraîche into the liquid after adding the butter. But make sure it doesn't come to the boil.**

Trout with rhubarb sauce

The tangy-sweet flavour of the rhubarb sauce perfectly offsets the richness of the trout, and can be used for other oily fish too – especially mackerel.

10 minutes preparation time
12 minutes cooking time
292 Kcal per portion
8g fat per portion of which
1.5g is saturated
4 servings

Rhubarb 450g (1lb), washed, trimmed and cut into 2.5cm (1in) pieces

Caster sugar 75g (3oz)

Orange 1 small, pared rind and juice

Rainbow trout 4, gutted and cleaned

Coarse sea salt and freshly ground black pepper

Lemons 2, 1 cut in half, the other cut into slices, to garnish

Lovage 4 sprigs (if unavailable, use celery leaves)

Parsley 4 large sprigs

Spring onion 1, trimmed, halved widthways and cut into long thin strips

1 Place the rhubarb, sugar and orange juice in a lidded saucepan. Cover and cook over a moderate heat until the rhubarb is soft and the juice flows. To drain, pour the rhubarb into a nylon or stainless steel sieve placed over a bowl.

2 Pour the rhubarb juice back into the saucepan, boil gently until reduced by about half and slightly syrupy, and then mix in the rhubarb. Keep the rhubarb warm or, if serving cold, allow to cool.

3 Preheat the oven to 220°C/425°F/Gas 7. Line a large baking tray with foil and lightly oil.

4 Season the inside of each trout with a little salt, pepper and a sprinkling of lemon juice, then fill with the lovage, parsley sprigs and spring onion. Close up and place the trout on the oiled foil, then scatter the shredded orange rind over the top, adding a light sprinkling of salt and a little more pepper.

5 Cover the trout with another sheet of oiled foil and fold in the edges to seal (if necessary, the trout can be cooked on two baking trays). Cook in the preheated oven for 10–12 minutes, until the trout's flesh turns opaque and flakes easily when tested with the tip of a knife.

6 Serve the cooked trout garnished with lemon slices and with the rhubarb sauce. Accompany with chunky chips and a crisp green salad.

Cook's tip

•The rhubarb sauce is just as good an accompaniment cold as hot, so prepare in advance if you prefer.

Chicken & root vegetable stir-fry

This is a delicious adaptation of a classic Chinese stir-fry, made with a colourful array of traditional British vegetables.

30 minutes preparation time
20 minutes cooking time
366 Kcal per portion
13.7g fat per portion of which
2.1g is saturated
3–4 servings

Skinless chicken breasts
2, totalling approximately
400g (14oz) total weight

Cornflour 1½ tbsp

Chicken stock 300ml
(½ pint)

Worcestershire sauce
3–4 tbsp

Tomato purée 1½ tbsp

Vegetable oil 3 tbsp

Celery 3 sticks, thinly
sliced

Onions 2, peeled, halved
and sliced widthways

Carrots 225g (8oz),
peeled and very thinly
sliced

Celeriac 400g (14oz)
piece, peeled and
coarsely grated

1 Cut each chicken breast in two horizontally, then cut into thin strips. In a small bowl, blend the cornflour with the chicken stock, Worcestershire sauce and tomato purée.

2 Heat 2 tbsp of the oil in a large wok or frying pan, add the chicken strips and stir-fry over a high heat for 3–4 minutes, or until the strips are opaque throughout. Remove from pan onto a plate and set aside.

3 Add the remaining oil to the wok, tip in all the vegetables and stir-fry over a high heat for about 5 minutes, until they are softened but still retain a crisp bite.

4 Return the chicken to the wok, including any juices remaining on the plate, add the cornflour mixture and bring to the boil, gently tossing the chicken and vegetables. Serve immediately with basmati rice.

Cook's tip
•**Instead of grating the celeriac, it can always be coarsely shredded in a food processor or mouli julienne.**

Chicken & corn pasties

These tasty pasties are perfect for a bonfire party or at a firework display. Serve hot if you are entertaining at home or cold if you are out and about.

1 hour preparation time
35 minutes cooking time
508 Kcal per portion
29.5g fat per portion of which
17.6g is saturated
6 pasties
Suitable for freezing, if frozen before baking

For the filling:
Skinless chicken breasts 2, totalling approximately 375g (13oz)

Chicken stock 600ml (1 pint)

Butter 25g (1oz)

Plain flour 25g (1oz)

Single or double cream 4 tbsp

Sweetcorn kernels 75g (3oz), canned or frozen

For the pastry:
Plain flour 225g (8oz)

Salt

Butter 110g (4oz)

Cheddar cheese 110g (4oz), grated

Egg 1 large, beaten with 1 tbsp cold water

Beaten egg or milk to glaze

Cook's tip
•**Any leftover sweetcorn used from a can can be kept and added to a salad or rice dish.**

1 To prepare the filling, place the chicken breasts in a saucepan, cover with the chicken stock and bring to the boil. Then reduce the heat and cook gently for 15–20 minutes until the flesh is opaque throughout – take care not to overcook, or the chicken will become tough. Leave to cool.

2 Remove the chicken breasts from the stock and drain well (reserving the stock). Cut into small dice, cover and put in the refrigerator while making the sauce.

3 Bring the chicken stock to the boil and cook gently until reduced to 300ml (½ pint). Melt the butter in another saucepan, stir in the flour and add the stock. Stirring continuously, bring the sauce to the boil, then reduce the heat and simmer for 2–3 minutes, stirring frequently.

4 Stir the cream, diced chicken and sweetcorn into the sauce, cover the surface closely with cling film (to prevent a skin forming) and chill while making the pastry.

5 To make the pastry, sift the flour and a pinch of salt into a mixing bowl and rub in the butter until the mixture resembles fine breadcrumbs. Mix in three-quarters of the cheese, add the egg and mix together, then knead the dough lightly on a floured surface to smooth. Wrap in cling film and chill for 10–15 minutes.

6 Preheat the oven to 220°C/425°F/ Gas 7. On a lightly floured surface, roll the dough out to approximately 3mm (⅛in) thick. Using a 15–18cm (6–7in) plate as a guide, cut out as many rounds as you can from the dough. Re-knead and re-roll the pastry trimmings and cut out more rounds, until you have 6 in total.

7 Turn the pastry rounds over so the floury sides are uppermost. Dividing the filling evenly, spoon it slightly off-centre on top of each pastry round. Brush the pastry edges with cold water and fold the wider half over the filling, pressing the edges firmly together to seal.

8 Create ridges around the pastry edges by lightly tapping with a knife. Place on one or two baking trays and brush with the beaten egg. Sprinkle evenly with the remaining cheese.

9 With a skewer, make a small hole in the top of each pasty to allow the steam to escape. Bake for 30–35 minutes until the pastry is cooked and golden brown. If necessary, towards the end of cooking, loosely cover the pasties with foil to prevent over-browning. Serve hot or cold.

A piping hot pastie wrapped in paper and held between warm woollen gloves is the perfect accompaniment to an evening by a bonfire. It will keep the cold at bay.

Chicken with ginger & coriander

A Thai-inspired chicken dish with subtle flavours. For best results, make it the day before and reheat, ensuring it is piping hot before serving.

30 minutes preparation time
1 hour cooking time plus overnight chilling, if serving next day
695 Kcal per portion
53.1g fat per portion of which
26.2g is saturated
4 servings

Chicken approximately 1.6kg (3½lb)

Butter 25g (1oz)

Olive oil 2 tbsp

Onions 350g (12oz), peeled, halved and quartered (if large, cut into eighths)

Garlic 2–3 cloves, peeled and crushed

Root ginger 50g (2oz), peeled and finely chopped

Plain flour 2 tbsp

Chicken stock 150ml (¼ pint)

Coconut cream 200ml carton

Chopped coriander 6–8 tbsp

Salt and freshly ground black pepper

Flaked almonds 25g (1oz), lightly toasted, to garnish

Paprika to garnish

Cook's tips

• **If serving this dish the next day, add the fresh coriander when reheating.**
• **A corn-fed chicken adds extra depth of flavour.**

1 With a very sharp knife, carefully remove the leg and thigh joints from each side of the bird. Cutting between the leg and thigh joint, divide each joint into 2 pieces.

2 Separate the breast from the backbone by cutting through the ribcage from the tail end with a pair of poultry shears or with a large sharp knife (the backbone will not be needed but can be used for stock). Cut the breast into two lengthways, then cut each piece in half widthways. You will now have 8 pieces of chicken.

3 Preheat the oven to 180°C/350°F/ Gas 4. Heat the butter and oil in a large flameproof, lidded casserole, add the chicken pieces and brown them lightly all over. Remove from the casserole and set aside.

4 Add the onions, garlic and ginger to the casserole and cook gently until they have softened, but not browned. Stir in the flour, add the stock and coconut cream and, stirring continuously, bring the casserole just up to the boil.

5 Return the chicken pieces to the pan and mix well with the sauce. Cover the surface closely with a sheet of non-stick baking paper, then cover with the lid. Cook in the oven for approximately 1 hour, or until the chicken is very tender, stirring the casserole occasionally.

6 Stir the chopped coriander into the chicken and season well. Scatter the toasted almonds over the top, sprinkle with paprika and serve accompanied with rice.

Lamb & aubergine pie

This pie takes its inspiration from both traditional British shepherd's pie and Greek moussaka. The result is a lovely combination of flavours with tender meat.

1 hour preparation time
50 minutes cooking time
615 Kcal per portion
41g fat per portion of which
19.9g is saturated
4 servings

Lamb 680g (1½lb) piece of lean leg or shoulder

Butter 75g (3oz)

Onion 1 large, peeled and chopped

Plain flour 2 tbsp

Tomatoes 350g (12oz), skinned (see Cook's Tip, page 158), halved, deseeded and roughly chopped

Mixed dried herbs 2–3 tsp

Chopped parsley 6 tbsp

Red wine 175ml (6fl oz)

Salt and freshly ground black pepper

Aubergine 1, sliced widthways

Olive oil 2–3 tbsp

Potatoes 1.12kg (2½lb), peeled and cubed

Milk 1–2 tbsp

Cream 2–3 tbsp double, single or crème fraîche

Egg 1 small, beaten

Flat-leaved parsley and paprika to garnish

Cook's tip

• **Prepare this pie a few hours, or a day, ahead and keep it covered in the refrigerator, ready for cooking when required.**

1 Remove all excess fat and tissue from the lamb, then cut the meat into 5mm (¼in) dice. Heat 50g (2oz) butter in a large, lidded frying pan. Add the lamb and cook over a moderately high heat until lightly browned. Do not let the butter burn. Remove from pan with a slotted spoon and set aside.

2 Add the onion to the pan and cook over a moderate heat until slightly softened, adding a little more butter if necessary.

3 Return the lamb to the pan and stir in the flour, then add the tomatoes, herbs, parsley and wine. Bring just up to the boil, reduce the heat, cover and simmer gently for 30 minutes, or until the meat is tender.

4 Preheat the grill to hot. Season the aubergine slices on both sides and brush lightly with the oil. Place on a foil-lined grill pan and cook under the grill for 2–3 minutes on each side, until lightly browned and softened, taking care not to overcook.

5 Meanwhile, put the potatoes into a lidded saucepan, cover with cold water, add a little salt and bring to the boil. Reduce the heat, partially cover and cook gently until softened but not broken up. Drain and mash with the remaining butter and milk and then add seasoning.

6 Preheat the oven to 200°C/400°F/ Gas 6. Stir the cream into the lamb mixture, then pour half into a deep, ovenproof dish, cover with aubergine slices, and then add the remaining lamb mixture.

7 Carefully spoon the mash over the lamb, spread evenly and mark into swirls with a palette knife – or decorate with a fork. Brush the mash with the beaten egg, place on a baking tray and cook in the centre of the oven for 45–50 minutes, until golden brown and bubbling hot. Garnish the pie with parsley and a light sprinkling of paprika and serve immediately with a crisp green salad or fine green beans.

Potato & smoked sausage bake

This rustic potato and sausage bake makes the perfect supper dish for a chilly evening in front of the fire.

30 minutes preparation time
1 hour 5 minutes cooking time
819 Kcal per portion
59.7g fat per portion of which **26.8g** is saturated
4 servings

Baking potatoes 900g (2lb), peeled and cut into 1cm (½in) dice

Onions 2 large, peeled and halved, each half cut into three lengthways and the wedges fanned

Smoked pork sausage rings 2 x 227g, each one cut into thick diagonal slices

Butter 50g (2oz), melted

Olive oil 2 tbsp

Mixed dried herbs 1–2 tsp

Salt and freshly ground black pepper

Single cream 4 tbsp

Cheddar cheese 75g (3oz), grated

Torn flat-leaved parsley to garnish

Cook's tips
•**Smoked pork sausage comes ready-cooked and you can find it in the supermarket near a fresh meat chiller cabinet.**
•**Serve the bake as it is or accompany it with a fresh, crisp green salad of watercress and lettuce, and with tomatoes if wished.**

1 Preheat the oven to 200°C/400°F/Gas 6. Put the potatoes into a large saucepan, cover with cold water and add a little salt. Bring to the boil and cook for 2 minutes. Pour into a colander and drain well.

2 Transfer the potatoes to a large baking dish, or small roasting tin, add the onions, sausage slices, butter, oil and herbs. Season lightly with salt and mix well. Cover with a lid or foil and bake for 45 minutes, stirring occasionally.

3 Remove the baking dish or roasting tin from the oven and uncover it. Drizzle the cream over the potato mixture, season with freshly ground black pepper and then sprinkle with the cheese.

4 Increase the oven temperature to 220°C/425°F/Gas 7. Return the potato and sausage bake to the oven and continue cooking for a further 15–20 minutes, or until golden brown and the potatoes are cooked. Serve hot, sprinkled with parsley.

Stilton-stuffed pork

The tangy, salty flavour of Stilton perfectly offsets the sweeter flavour of the pork tenderloin in this recipe.

20 minutes preparation time
40 minutes cooking time
402 Kcal per portion
20g fat per portion of which
11.2g is saturated
4 servings

Pork tenderloin 450g (1lb), trimmed

Stilton cheese 110g (4oz)

Plain flour 2 tbsp

Salt and freshly ground black pepper

Butter 25g (1oz)

Onion 1, peeled and sliced

Dessert apples 2, diced

White wine 125ml (4fl oz)

Chicken stock 125ml (4fl oz)

Natural yogurt 150g (5oz)

1 Preheat the oven to 180°C/350°F/ Gas 4. Cut the tenderloin into 4 equal pieces and beat into thin escalopes by placing each piece between two sheets of cling film. Using a wooden meat mallet or a rolling pin, beat out each escalope until it is approximately 3mm (⅛in) thick.

2 Cut the Stilton into 4 slices and place one piece on each pork escalope. Roll up and secure with a cocktail stick.

3 Place the flour on a plate, add seasoning and lightly coat the pork in the flour, shaking off the excess. Heat the butter in a frying pan until it is sizzling hot and fry the pork and onion together gently until they are lightly browned. Drain and transfer to a lidded casserole dish and add the chopped apples.

4 Drain off excess fat from frying pan, pour in the wine and stock and bring to the boil, stirring and scraping the browned residue from the bottom of the pan, then strain through a sieve (to remove any browned pieces) into the casserole.

5 Cover the surface closely with non-stick baking paper, then cover with a tightly fitting lid and bake in the oven for 40 minutes, or until the pork is cooked through and tender.

6 Remove the cocktail sticks from the pork olives, then arrange them on warm serving plates. Blend the yogurt into the sauce and pour over the pork. Serve with sugar snap peas and sliced leeks, steamed and tossed with chopped parsley.

Cook's tip
•**Don't worry if some of the Stilton escapes when you are cooking the pork. It adds to the flavour of the sauce.**

Roast pork with fruity sauces

Blackberries add a delicious autumn twist to this very British Sunday roast. Pick wild blackberries if you can as these will have the very best flavour.

30 minutes preparation time
1 hour 50 minutes cooking time
419 Kcal per portion
12.1g fat per portion of which
4.2g is saturated
6 servings

Pork loin roast, a six-bone piece approximately 1.8kg (4lb), ready prepared with the top 2.5cm (1in) trimmed of rind and fat, bones scraped clean, the remaining rind scored
Olive oil 2 tbsp
Salt and freshly ground black pepper
Cooking apples 450g (1lb), peeled, cored and sliced
Blackberries 225g (8oz), hulled, washed and dried
Caster sugar 110g (4oz)
Lemon 1 large, strained juice only

Cook's tips
• **Carving is made easier if the crackling/pork rind is removed before taking the loin to the table.**
• **If using a roasting dish that is not flameproof, pour the apple and blackberry juice into the dish and stir well with the roasting juices, then strain into a saucepan, bring to the boil and boil gently until reduced.**

1 Preheat the oven to 220°C/425°F/ Gas 7. Coat the scored pork rind with the oil, then sprinkle generously with salt and rub it well into the cuts. Place the pork in a roasting tin and cook it in the centre of the oven for 15–20 minutes to help the rind form a crisp crackling.

2 Reduce the oven temperature to 180°C/350°F/Gas 4 and continue cooking for 1¼–1½ hours, basting frequently, until the pork is richly browned (but not burnt), has formed a crisp crackling and there is no sign of any pink juices when the flesh is pierced with a small pointed knife. If over-browning, cover loosely with foil.

3 Meanwhile, place the apples and blackberries in separate, lidded saucepans. Add 75g (3oz) of the sugar and the lemon juice to the apples, the remaining sugar to the blackberries. Cover both pans. Cook the apples for 15–20 minutes until soft and fluffy and the blackberries for 8–10 minutes, until softened but not broken up.

4 Strain the juice from both fruits, mix together and reserve. Gently fold together the fluffy apples and blackberries, transfer to a serving dish, cover and set aside.

5 When the pork is done, transfer to a serving plate, loosely cover with foil and leave to rest.

6 To make the sauce, skim all the excess fat from the juices left in the roasting tin. Pour the reserved blackberry and apple juice into the tin and bring to the boil over a moderate heat, stirring and scraping the residue from the bottom of the tin.

7 Reduce the heat under the roasting tin and allow the sauce to bubble gently, stirring frequently, until reduced and slightly thickened. Season with salt and pepper, then strain into a gravy boat or jug.

8 Serve the pork accompanied with the cooked apple and blackberry mixture, and with the apple and blackberry sauce. To carve, cut between the bones with a sharp knife (but see also Cook's Tip).

Cutting the pork into pieces like this and piling them high on a heated serving plate is a fabulous way to present this dish at a supper party.

Beef & bean casserole

This rich 'beefy' casserole is made with fresh beans – runner beans and French green beans – plus fresh tomatoes. A comforting combination.

20 minutes preparation time
2½ hours cooking time
548 Kcal per portion
24.7g fat per portion of which
9.4g is saturated
4–6 servings
Suitable for freezing

Butter 25g (1oz)

Olive oil 2 tbsp

Shallots 350g (12oz), peeled

Braising steak 900g (2lb), trimmed of excess fat (if necessary), cut into 2.5cm (1in) cubes

Plain flour 2 tbsp

Mixed dried herbs 1–2 tsp

Red wine 225ml (8fl oz)

Good-quality beef stock 300ml (½ pint)

Runner beans 350g (12oz), trimmed and cut into thick pieces diagonally

French beans 225g (8oz), topped and tailed

Large tomatoes 450g (1lb), skinned (see Cook's Tip, page 158), quartered and deseeded

Cook's tips

•**For the best flavour and succulence, choose good-quality, lean braising or chuck steak.**
•**Choose fatter green French beans, as these are less likely to break up during cooking.**

1 Preheat the oven to 180°C/350°F/Gas 4. Place the butter and oil in a large, flameproof, lidded casserole and heat together until hot. Then add the shallots, reduce the heat to moderate and cook, stirring frequently, until the shallots are lightly browned.

2 Remove the shallots from the casserole onto a plate and set aside. In batches, lightly brown the meat to seal, removing each batch from the casserole when browned. Return all the meat to the dish and stir in the flour and herbs. Add the wine and stock and bring to the boil, continuing to stir.

3 Move the casserole from the heat, and return the shallots to the pan – including any juices remaining on the plate. Add the runner beans, French beans and tomatoes. Mix well, return to the heat and bring back to the boil.

4 Remove the casserole from the heat and cover the surface closely with a sheet of non-stick baking or greaseproof paper. Cover the casserole with the lid, transfer to the oven and cook for 2–2½ hours until the meat is tender and the vegetables are cooked.

5 Remove the paper covering and serve the casserole immediately, accompanied with warm crusty bread or creamy mashed potatoes.

Fresh tomato sauce

This is the ideal way to make good use of a glut of tomatoes. It is perfect for freezing, so make plenty for use through the winter.

30 minutes preparation time
45 minutes cooking time plus cooling, if freezing
107 Kcal per portion
6.3g fat per portion of which
0.9g is saturated
6 servings
Suitable for freezing
Suitable for vegetarians

Ripe tomatoes 1.3kg (3lb), washed and dried

Olive oil 3 tbsp

Onions 225g (8oz), peeled and finely chopped

Basil leaves large bunch, approximately 25g (1oz), shredded

Finely chopped parsley 25g (1oz)

Caster sugar 1–2 tsp

Salt and freshly ground black pepper

1 With a small, sharp-pointed knife, remove the centre core from each tomato (see Cook's Tip, page 108), then place in a large heatproof bowl. Cover the tomatoes with boiling water, leave for 1–2 minutes, then pour into a large colander and drain well. Remove the skins, cut each tomato in half and remove the seeds.

2 Heat the oil in a large, lidded saucepan. Add the onions and cook them over a moderate to low heat until softened, but not browned, stirring frequently.

3 Roughly chop the tomatoes and add to the onions, along with the basil, parsley and sugar. Cover and cook gently for about 45 minutes until the tomatoes begin to soften, then remove the lid and continue cooking until the mixture thickens and there is no watery liquid left on the surface. Stir frequently to prevent the mixture from burning. Season the sauce and leave to cool.

Cook's tip

•The sauce can be left chunky or puréed to make it smoother. It can be served with omelettes, chicken, meat and fish. Or add it to soups, casseroles or stews to give them a richer flavour.

Beetroot & apple chutney

Autumn is the perfect time for making chutneys, particularly for gardeners, who often end up with more homegrown vegetables than they can actually use!

1 hour preparation time
4 hours cooking time
30 minutes potting time
60 Kcal per portion
0.1g fat per portion of which
0g is saturated
2.25kg (5lb) approximately
Suitable for vegetarians

Raw beetroot 1.3kg (3lb), peeled and coarsely grated

Cooking apples 900g (2lb), peeled, cored and roughly chopped

Onions 680g (1½lb), peeled and chopped

Sultanas 225g (8oz)

Seedless raisins 225g (8oz)

Salt 1 level tbsp

Pink peppercorns in brine 1 tbsp, drained and crushed

Allspice berries 2 tbsp, finely ground

Mixed ground spice 2–3 tsp

Light muscovado sugar 500g (1lb 2oz)

Granulated sugar 250g (9oz)

Root ginger 50g (2oz), peeled and grated

Coarsely ground black pepper 1 tsp

Distilled malt vinegar 5% acidity 900ml (1½ pints)

Clean jars preferably with screw-top lids

Waxed paper discs and, if without lids, cellophane jam jar covers

1 Put all the prepared ingredients into a large preserving pan. Place over a moderate heat and cook, stirring occasionally, until the sugar is completely dissolved.

2 Bring the chutney up to a gentle boil and allow to bubble, stirring frequently, until the mixture is reduced and thickened. The consistency is right when the chutney is slow to join up when a spoon is drawn through the centre, and there is virtually no excess liquid on the top.

3 Fill clean, warm jars with the chutney – right to the top, as it will shrink a little as it cools. Place a waxed paper disc, waxed side down, on the hot chutney. Cover the jars loosely with kitchen paper or a clean tea towel and leave to cool until completely cold.

4 When the chutney is cold, wipe the jars clean with a damp cloth (if necessary), and then cover with clean, screw-top lids or with cellophane jam pot covers.

5 Label the chutney and store in a cool, dark, dry and airy cupboard for 2–3 months before using. This will allow the chutney to mature and mellow in flavour (losing the sharp, acidic flavour it has when first made).

Cook's tips
•To prevent staining hands when peeling and grating beetroot, wear thin, clean rubber gloves. If you do get your hands stained, rubbing with a cut lemon helps to remove the colour.
•Grating the beetroot in a food processor helps to speed up the preparation time. If preferred, the apples and onions may also be grated in a food processor.

Chutneys are a fine addition in
any kitchen cupboard. Use them
to liven up bland dishes, serve
with cheese or in sandwiches.

Apples & pears in cider

Homegrown Cox's apples and Comice pears together with English cider make the perfect trio for this lovely dessert. Serve it hot or cold, as preferred.

40 minutes preparation time
40 minutes cooking time
518 Kcal per portion
24.3g fat per portion of which
15.1g is saturated
6 servings
Suitable for freezing
Suitable for vegetarians

Strong, dry cider 1 litre (1¾ pints)

Lemons 3, finely pared rind cut into strips and juice

Orange 2, finely pared rind cut into strips and juice

Cinnamon stick 15cm (6in) piece

Whole cloves 6–8

Whole cardamom pods 12

Demerara sugar 175g (6oz)

Dessert apples 6, peeled, stalks left on

Ripe pears 6, peeled, stalks left on

Double cream 300ml (½ pint)

Caster sugar 1 tsp

Vanilla extract 1 tsp

Ground cinnamon 1 tsp

1 Pour the cider into a very large saucepan, add the lemon and orange rind and juice, the spices and sugar. Bring slowly to the boil, stirring occasionally, until the sugar dissolves.

2 With the tip of a small, pointed knife, remove the calyx from each apple and pear – it is like removing a small cone shape from the base.

3 Place the apples and pears in the cider, ensuring they are well covered, then cover the pan and cook gently for 35–40 minutes, until translucent and the tip of the knife goes in easily. Gently turn the fruit several times during cooking and do not allow the cider to boil or the fruit will break up.

4 When cooked, carefully remove the apples and pears from the cider with a slotted spoon and place in a large serving bowl. Then remove the orange and lemon rind, and the spices, and add to the fruit (keep warm if serving hot).

5 Bring the cider to the boil and simmer gently until it has reduced by two-thirds and is slightly syrupy. Pour over the fruit and serve hot or leave to cool, then cover and refrigerate.

6 Just before serving, whip the cream with caster sugar, vanilla extract and ground cinnamon – just until it forms soft peaks. Transfer to a serving dish to accompany the cooked fruit.

This is a modern twist for the classic combination of succulent, sweet fruit and soft, whipped cream. And, wow, does it look stylish!

Cook's tip

•**If serving cold, the apples and pears can be cooked 2–3 days beforehand and stored, covered, in the refrigerator.**

Rhubarb syllabub trifle

Rhubarb combined with a fluffy lemon syllabub gives this trifle a slight tartness, making it a refreshing change to the traditional rich and creamy version.

1 hour preparation time
2 hours or overnight chilling time
580 Kcal per portion
23.4g fat per portion of which
14.4g is saturated
6 servings
Suitable for vegetarians

Lemon 1 large, a little grated rind to garnish and the rest finely pared and strained juice

Caster sugar 250g (9oz)

White wine 150ml (¼ pint)

Rhubarb 900g (2lb), washed, trimmed and cut into 2.5cm (1in) pieces

Trifle sponge cakes 1 packet of 8

Raspberry jam approximately 175g (6oz)

Double cream 284ml carton

Finely sliced pistachio nuts optional

Cook's tip

•**Preferably choose younger stalks of rhubarb and those with the reddest colour. Younger stalks are more tender, whereas older ones can be stringy and drier. Redder stalks also give the trifle a better colour.**

1 Place the pared lemon rind and juice and 75g (3oz) of the sugar in a bowl. Add the white wine and stir until dissolved. Cover and chill.

2 Put the rhubarb into a wide, stainless steel, lidded frying pan or flameproof casserole. Sprinkle with the remaining sugar and add 2–3 tbsp of cold water. Cover and cook over a moderate heat until the rhubarb juices flow, and the fruit is softened but not broken up. Remove from the heat, carefully drain and reserve the juice.

3 Slice each sponge cake in half horizontally. Spread jam over half of the slices, then cover with the remaining slices and place, in a single layer, in six individual glasses, trimming the sponge to fit. Spread any remaining jam over the top of the sponge cakes.

4 Spoon approximately two-thirds of the rhubarb juice over the sponge cakes. Use enough to moisten them well, but not to saturate. (Any left-over juice can be chilled and diluted with soda or tonic water to make a refreshing drink.)

5 Spoon the cooked rhubarb over the sponge cakes, cover and refrigerate until cold.

6 To make the topping, remove the lemon rind from the wine and discard. Then pour the cream into the wine and whisk until it is thick enough to hold a trail – but take care not to over-whisk or the mixture will curdle.

7 Pour the syllabub on top of the chilled rhubarb and mark with a deep swirl. Cover the glasses and put in the refrigerator to chill for at least 2 hours, or even overnight. Serve scattered with pistachio nuts, if using, and grated lemon rind.

Blackberry & apple oat crumble

What better way to enjoy autumn fruits than in a crumble? The porridge oats add extra crunch and blackberries an extra tanginess.

10 minutes preparation time
1 hour cooking time
371 Kcal per portion
13.4g fat per portion of which
8g is saturated
6 servings
Suitable for vegetarians

Cooking apples 680g
(1½lb), peeled and sliced
Blackberries 200g (7oz)
Granulated sugar 110g
(4oz)
Wholemeal flour 100g
(3½oz)
Butter 90g (3½oz)
Light muscovado sugar
50g (2oz)
Porridge oats 100g
(3½oz)

1 Preheat the oven to 190°C/375°F/ Gas 5 and put the fruit into a 1.25 litre (2 pint) ovenproof dish in layers with the granulated sugar.

2 Place the flour in a separate bowl and rub in the butter until the mixture resembles fine breadcrumbs. Stir in the brown sugar and porridge oats.

3 Sprinkle the crumble mixture thickly and evenly over the fruit, pressing down lightly.

4 Place the crumble on a baking tray and cook in the oven for 15 minutes. Reduce the temperature to 180°C/ 350°F/Gas 4 and continue cooking for a further 45 minutes or until the top is lightly browned. Serve the crumble hot with custard.

Cook's tip
•If you pick wild blackberries from the hedgerows, be sure to pick those that are well away from any busy main roads to ensure they are not contaminated by car exhaust fumes, and wash them well before eating.

Cumberland apple plate cake

To most of us, a fruit pie with a double crust made on a plate is known as a 'fruit pie', but in Cumbria it's known as a 'plate cake'. Try this delicious version.

1 hour preparation time
1 hour 10 minutes cooking time
823 Kcal per slice
32.5g fat per slice of which
19.2g is saturated
8 slices
Suitable for vegetarians

Plain flour 350g (12oz), plus 15g (½oz)
Salt
Caster sugar 50g (2oz), plus extra for sprinkling
Butter 175g (6oz), cubed
Eggs 2 large, beaten
Cooking apples 3 large, totalling approximately 800g (1¾lb)
Dessert apples 3 large, Cox's or Golden Delicious, totalling approximately 450g (1lb)
Light muscovado sugar 200g (7oz)
Lemon 1, finely grated rind and strained juice

Cook's tips
•**If you like your apple pie spicy, add a teaspoon of mixed spice or ground cinnamon and a few whole cloves to the apple mixture.**
•**Halved and stoned plums or damsons can be used instead of the dessert apples.**

1 To make the pastry, sift the 350g (12oz) of flour, a pinch of salt and the caster sugar into a large mixing bowl, add the butter and rub it into the flour until the mixture resembles breadcrumbs, and then make a well in the centre.

2 Pour the beaten eggs into the well and mix with a round-bladed knife to make a soft, but not sticky, dough. Turn the dough onto a lightly floured surface and knead gently until smooth. Wrap in cling film and chill while preparing the apples.

3 Peel and core both types of apple, then cut into quarters and slice thinly into a large bowl. Add the remaining flour, brown sugar, lemon rind and juice, and mix together gently. This is most easily done with your hands.

4 Preheat the oven to 220°C/425°F/ Gas 7 and place a large baking sheet in the centre of the oven. Meanwhile, roll out half of the chilled pastry into a circle large enough to cover a 25cm (10in) ovenproof plate with raised edges (or a shallow, ovenproof dish). Cover the plate with the pastry, allowing the excess to overhang the edges of the plate.

5 Spoon all of the prepared apple mixture onto the lined plate, piling quite high. Roll out the remaining pastry into a circle large enough to completely cover the pie. Brush the edges of the pastry on the plate with cold water, then cover the pie with the pastry.

6 Press the pastry edges firmly together to seal, then trim and decorate the edge by 'pinching' with your forefinger and thumb. Make a small hole in the centre of the pie with a skewer.

7 Re-knead and re-roll the pastry trimmings, cut into leaves, moisten with cold water and arrange them, overlapping, in a circle just above the 'pinched' edge.

8 Place the pie on the hot baking tray and bake for 30 minutes, then reduce the oven temperature to 190°C/375°F/ Gas 5 and continue cooking for another 30–40 minutes, until the apples are cooked (when tested with a skewer inserted through the hole in the top of the pie) and the pastry is golden brown. If necessary, cover the pie with a sheet of foil to prevent over-browning. Serve the pie hot, accompanied with Cumberland rum butter, whipped cream or ice cream.

Why not try apple and dried apricots or
raisins, rhubarb and ginger, or summer fruits?
All of these make great comfort food!

Plum streusel tart

Streusel is a German sweet topping, rather like a crumble. Here it is made with added oats and demerara sugar for a crunchier texture.

50 minutes preparation time
45 minutes cooking time
545 Kcal per portion
31.3g fat per portion of which
16.1g is saturated
6 servings
Suitable for vegetarians

Plain flour 200g (7oz)

Icing sugar 40g (1½oz), plus a little extra for sifting

Ground almonds or ground lightly toasted hazelnuts 50g (2oz)

Unsalted butter 175g (6oz)

Egg 1, beaten

Rolled oats 75g (3oz)

Demerara sugar 50g (2oz)

Mixed ground spice 1 tsp

Lemon 1, finely grated rind only

Redcurrant jelly 2–3 tbsp

Plums 8–10, depending on size, halved and stoned and cut into quarters if very large

Double cream whipped, to serve

Cook's tip
•**If wished, make the pastry the day before and line the flan tin ready to be filled and baked when required the following day. Cover and refrigerate until using.**

1 Sift 110g (4oz) of the flour and all the icing sugar into a large mixing bowl. Add and mix in the ground almonds or hazelnuts, and rub in 75g (3oz) of the butter until the mixture resembles fine breadcrumbs. Add the beaten egg and mix to make a soft, but not sticky, dough.

2 Turn the dough onto a lightly floured surface, knead gently until smooth, and then roll out into a circle large enough to line a 25cm (10in) loose-bottomed, fluted flan tin or dish.

3 Line the tin (or dish) with the pastry and press it into the flutes. Trim the edge and chill.

4 Preheat the oven to 190°C/375°F/ Gas 5. Make the topping by sifting the remaining flour into a bowl and mixing in the oats, demerara sugar, spice and lemon rind. Rub the remaining butter into the mixture until it resembles breadcrumbs.

5 Place the lined flan tin on a baking tray and spread the redcurrant jelly evenly over the bottom. Arrange the plums, cut sides uppermost, on top of the jam.

6 Sprinkle the streusel mixture evenly over the plums and press gently to firm and make level. Bake for 40–45 minutes until the streusel topping is golden brown and the plums are softened.

7 Remove the cooked tart from the oven, sift icing sugar evenly over the top and serve either hot or cold, accompanied with whipped cream or vanilla ice cream.

Fresh pear shortcake

The sweet, silky taste of the pears works perfectly with the soft cheese in this recipe. The crumbly base adds an interesting texture.

25 minutes preparation time
1 hour 15 minutes cooking time
410 Kcal per portion
27.4g fat per portion of which
16.8g is saturated
6 servings
Suitable for vegetarians

Self-raising flour 150g (5oz)

Ground rice 25g (1oz)

Lemon 1, grated rind and juice

Dark muscovado sugar 50g (2oz)

Butter 150g (5oz)

Pears 2, peeled, cored and halved

Full fat soft cheese 110g (4oz)

Egg 1

Natural almond essence a few drops

Flaked almonds to decorate, optional

Icing sugar for dusting

Crème fraîche optional

Cook's tip

• **To speed up the preparation of this recipe, the shortcake base may be prepared, covered and refrigerated 1–2 days before required – or even frozen.**

1 Preheat the oven to 190°C/375°F/ Gas 5. In a bowl, mix together the flour, ground rice, lemon rind and sugar. Rub in the butter until the mixture resembles fine breadcrumbs, then lightly work together to form a soft ball of dough.

2 Press the dough into a lightly greased 20cm (8in) loose-bottomed, fluted flan tin and prick well. Bake in the oven for 20–25 minutes until only just lightly browned.

3 Starting at the stalk end of each pear half and 1cm (½in) from the top, cut into slices approximately 3mm (⅛in) thick. Place each pear half on the shortcake, fanning out the slices. Sprinkle with lemon juice.

4 Beat together the cream cheese, egg and almond essence until smooth. Spoon over the pears and shortcake, sprinkle with the flaked almonds, if using, and bake at 180°C/350°F/Gas 4 for 40–50 minutes, until golden. Sift icing sugar lightly over the top and serve hot or cold with crème fraîche, if liked.

Luxury Eccles cakes

Eccles cakes are quick and easy to make and, when eaten warm, are the perfect treat to banish those 'November Blues'!

20 minutes preparation time
15 minutes cooking time
252 Kcal per cake
13.2g fat per cake of which
6g is saturated
12 cakes
Suitable for vegetarians

Luxury blend mixed dried fruits 175g (6oz)

Dark muscovado sugar 50g (2oz)

Mixed ground spice 1 tsp

Nutmeg ½ tsp freshly grated

Lemons 2, finely grated rind only

Brandy, sherry or rum 2 tbsp

Butter 40g (1½oz), melted

Puff pastry 500g packet

Egg 1, beaten

Caster sugar for sifting

1 Preheat the oven to 220°C/425°F/ Gas 7. In a large bowl, mix together the dried fruits, sugar, spices, lemon rind, chosen spirit and the butter.

2 On a lightly floured surface, roll out the pastry to 3mm (⅛in) thick. Using a 9cm (3½in) plain round cutter, stamp as many rounds as you can from the pastry and set aside.

3 Re-fold the pastry trimmings, in layers, and then re-roll and stamp out more rounds until you have 12.

4 Dividing evenly, place a rounded teaspoonful of the fruit mixture in the centre of each pastry circle. Brush the edges with cold water, then bring up and over the filling and pinch firmly together to seal.

5 Turn the filled pastry rounds over and then roll out gently into neat 7.5cm (3in) circles.

6 Place the Eccles cakes on greased baking trays and brush lightly with beaten egg, then lightly score the tops, diagonally, three times. Bake for 12–15 minutes until well risen, golden brown and crisp to the touch.

7 Sift the Eccles cakes with caster sugar while they are still hot. Eat warm, or leave until cold.

Eccles cakes are a northern delicacy. Play around with the recipe by using cinnamon instead of mixed spice, and substitute currants for the mixed fruit.

Cook's tip
• **Eccles cakes stored in an airtight tin will keep well for several days. They are just as tasty cold as hot.**

Ginger muffins

Muffins are at their best when freshly cooked and still warm. Bake a batch on Halloween to give to 'trick or treaters' who may call.

10 minutes preparation time
20 minutes cooking time
191 Kcal per muffin
9.3g fat per muffin of which
5.7g is saturated
24 muffins
Suitable for freezing
Suitable for vegetarians

Paper cake cases 24
Egg 1
Caster sugar 200g (7oz)
Plain flour 350g (12oz)
Baking powder 1½ tsp
Ground ginger 2 tsp
Ground cinnamon 1½ tsp
Ground nutmeg ½ tsp
Butter 225g (8oz)
Black treacle 175g (6oz)
Milk 125ml (4fl oz)
Soured cream 125ml (4fl oz)

1 Preheat the oven to 180°C/350°F/ Gas 4. Line two bun tin trays with paper cases. In a bowl, whisk together the egg and sugar until fluffy. Sift the dry ingredients into a large bowl and make a well in the centre.

2 Melt the butter and treacle together in a small pan, cool a little and then stir into the dry ingredients along with the egg mixture.

3 Bring the milk to the boil and stir into the mixture, then add and blend in the soured cream.

4 Spoon the muffin mixture into paper cases, dividing evenly, and bake for 20 minutes, until well risen, firm and springy to the touch. Cool on a wire rack.

Cook's tips

•To cook larger, American-style muffins, use a deeper muffin tin, as the ordinary bun tin will be too shallow.
•Chocolate chunks and chopped brazil nuts are an alternative filling.

Cranberry cup

Quick to make, this punch is just the thing to serve on Bonfire Night. For a non-alcoholic version, substitute the red wine with extra cranberry juice.

20 minutes preparation time
20 minutes cooking time
229 Kcal per portion
0.3g fat per portion of which
0g is saturated
6 servings
Suitable for vegetarians

Cranberry juice 1 litre carton

Red wine 1 x 70cl bottle (or 2 bottles if serving a larger number of people)

Brandy, rum or whisky 150ml (5fl oz), optional

Oranges 2 large, juice of 1, the other thinly sliced

Lemons 2, juice of 1, the other thinly sliced

Lime 1, thinly sliced

Granulated or caster sugar 75g (3oz)

Cardamom pods 12

Cloves 8 – studded into 2 slices of the orange

Cinnamon stick 15cm (6in) piece

Vanilla bean 1

Kiwi fruit 1, peeled and thinly sliced

Star fruit 1, ribs trimmed with a vegetable peeler, then thinly sliced

Cook's tips
•**Do not allow the punch to boil as this will cause a scum to form and can make the spices bitter.**
•**A stainless steel preserving pan is just perfect for making large amounts of hot punch.**

1 Pour the cranberry juice, wine and chosen spirit, if using, into a large stainless steel saucepan.

2 Add the prepared oranges, lemons, lime, sugar, spices and the vanilla bean. Bring slowly just up to the boil, stirring until the sugar dissolves. Reduce the heat and simmer gently for 15 minutes – to allow the flavour of the spices to permeate throughout.

3 Just before serving, float the kiwi fruit and star fruit slices on top of the punch. Serve in heatproof punch cups or heatproof glasses.

Plum jam

For a real morning treat, smother your hot buttered toast with this wonderful jam. It can also be made with damsons or greengages.

1½–2 hours cooking time
86 Kcal per rounded tbsp
0g fat per rounded tbsp
2.25–2.7kg (5–6lb) jam
Suitable for vegetarians

Firm, ripe plums 1.8kg (4lb), washed

Preserving sugar 1.8kg (4lb)

Clean jam jars preferably with screw-top lids

Waxed paper discs and, if without lids, cellophane jam jar covers

Cook's tips

•**The yield will depend on the variety of plum used – those with a tart, sharper flavour such as Czars and damsons will give a higher yield than sweeter plums, such as Victoria.**
•**If you do not have a preserving pan or very large saucepan (one that will allow the jam to boil without boiling over), make in two batches. To allow room for vigorous boiling, have the pan only half full when the sugar has been added.**

1 Place the plums in a preserving pan or a large stainless steel saucepan. (If you prefer, halve and stone the plums before cooking; however, if you leave them whole, the stones will come to the surface during boiling, and can be easily skimmed off – see step 4.) Add 300ml (½ pint) water and cook over a moderate heat until the juices flow freely and the plums are very soft. Stir frequently with a large wooden spoon (be sure not to use one that has been used when cooking onions!).

2 Add the sugar and stir until it is completely dissolved. Then bring to a full rolling boil and cook for 10–12 minutes, or until a set is reached (see step 3). Put the jam jars in a low oven to warm.

3 To test for a set, spoon a little of the jam onto a cold saucer, refrigerate for a few minutes until cold, then push the jam with a finger – if it wrinkles, the jam is ready. If not, continue boiling – and test for a set every 2–3 minutes.

4 When the jam has reached setting point, remove from heat and leave to settle for 2–3 minutes, then skim off all the scum and stones (if not stones not already removed) from the surface.

5 Carefully pour the hot jam into the warmed jars and place a waxed paper disc, wax side down, on the surface. Cover immediately with cellophane covers or leave until completely cold and then cover. Store in a cool, dry, airy cupboard.

The great thing about home-made jam is that it is not packed with extra preservatives – and it tastes so good, you won't need to keep it for very long!

Winter

Roasted red pepper soup

The rich, red colour of this soup is so attractive that it's perfect to serve when entertaining. It also tastes good chilled and sprinkled with sliced olives.

15 minutes preparation time
40 minutes cooking time
251 Kcal per portion
20.1g fat per portion of which
7.7g is saturated
4 servings
Suitable for freezing
Suitable for vegetarians

Red peppers 4, halved and deseeded

Olive oil 3–4 tbsp

Butter 50g (2oz)

Onions 2, peeled and chopped

Vegetable stock cubes 2

Water 1 litre (1¾ pints)

Salt and freshly ground black pepper

Chopped basil 1–2 tbsp, plus tiny leaves to garnish

1 Preheat the grill to hot. Spread the peppers out, skin side up, on a baking sheet and brush over half of the oil. Cook them under the grill for about 10 minutes, until the skins start to char, then turn over and brush the remaining oil over the pepper flesh.

2 Cook for a further 3–5 minutes, until the flesh starts to turn golden. Remove the peppers from under the grill and place the halves in a plastic bag. Leave the peppers to cool, then remove them and peel off the skins and discard. Roughly chop the pepper flesh, reserving a few slices for garnishing.

3 Heat the butter in a lidded saucepan. Add the onions and cook over a gentle heat for 7–10 minutes, until they starts to soften but not colour. Then add the pepper flesh to the pan and cook for a further 2–3 minutes.

4 Crumble the stock cubes into the pan and pour in the water. Bring the mixture to the boil, then cover the pan, reduce the heat and simmer gently for 20 minutes.

5 Transfer to a blender or food processor and purée until smooth, in batches if necessary. Season to taste and stir in the chopped basil just before serving.

6 Pour into warmed serving dishes and garnish with the pepper slices, basil leaves and some freshly ground black pepper.

Cook's tips
•The cold soup may be poured into a freezer-proof container and frozen for up to 1 month.
•Placing the peppers in a plastic bag as soon as they've been grilled makes them easy to peel.

Green vegetable soup

This fresh-tasting soup is truly delicious and, when served with warm crusty bread to mop up the juices, makes a great snack or starter.

10 minutes preparation time
25 minutes cooking time
108 Kcal per portion
6.8g fat per portion of which
3.4g is saturated
4 servings
Suitable for vegetarians

Butter 25g (1oz)

Leek 1, washed and sliced

Celery 2 sticks, washed and sliced

Garlic 1 clove, peeled and crushed

Water 1 litre (1¾ pints)

Vegetable stock cubes 2

Frozen peas 110g (4oz)

Savoy cabbage ½ small cabbage, finely shredded

Chopped parsley 2 tbsp

Salt and freshly ground black pepper

1 Melt the butter in a large, lidded saucepan. Add the leek and celery and cook, stirring, for 4–5 minutes, until soft but not brown.

2 Add the garlic and cook for a further 1–2 minutes. Add the water and bring to the boil, then crumble the stock cubes into the pan and stir until dissolved. Cover and simmer for 10 minutes.

3 Add the peas, then place the cabbage on top, without stirring it in, so that it steams. Cook for another 5–8 minutes, uncovered, until the vegetables are just tender. To serve, stir the cabbage into the soup and add parsley and seasoning to taste.

Cook's tip
•Any green vegetables in season will work well in this recipe, such as finely shredded Brussel sprouts or pak choi, which may be used in place of the Savoy cabbage.

Cream of chestnut soup

This smooth, creamy soup is delicious with the bacon garnish or with finely chopped ham. For a vegetarian dish, sprinkle it with some chopped herbs.

5 minutes preparation time
55 minutes cooking time
253 Kcal per portion
18.6g fat per portion of which
10.9g is saturated
6 servings
Suitable for freezing

Butter 25g (1oz)

Onion 1 small, peeled and chopped

Chestnuts 1–2 x 240g cans or 200g packets, vacuum packed

Chicken stock 600ml (1 pint)

Milk 300ml (½ pint)

Salt and freshly ground black pepper

Double cream 150ml (¼ pint)

Streaky bacon rashers 3, grilled and cut into strips for garnishing

1 Melt the butter in a large, lidded saucepan, add the onion and cook it over a medium heat for 3–4 minutes until it starts to soften but not colour.

2 Reserve three of the chestnuts for garnishing, add the rest to the pan with the onion and allow to cook for 1–2 minutes.

3 Pour the stock into the pan, bring to the boil then reduce the heat, cover the saucepan and cook gently for 45 minutes. Transfer to a blender or food processor and purée until smooth, in batches if necessary.

4 Return the soup to the saucepan, then add the milk and seasoning and reheat gently.

5 Serve the soup in individual, warmed bowls garnished with swirls of cream, snipped bacon rashers and crumbled chestnuts.

Cook's tip

•If you want to use fresh chestnuts, then place 450g (1lb) of them in a saucepan. Cover with cold water and bring to the boil. Reduce the heat and simmer for about 5 minutes. Remove the pan from the heat and drain the chestnuts. Leave them until they are cool enough to handle, then remove and discard the shells and inner skins.

Soup is such an adaptable dish.
You can add so many things to play
with the flavour. Try mushroom
seasoning, a glass of Madeira,
or a dash of Worcestershire sauce.

Winter vegetable soup

This soup is ideal for using up any leftover vegetables – just make up the weight of vegetables with any that you have already.

5 minutes preparation time
40 minutes cooking time
243 Kcal per portion
12.8g fat per portion of which
7.3g is saturated
4 servings
Suitable for freezing
Suitable for vegetarians

Butter 50g (2oz)

Onion 1, peeled and sliced

Parsnips 225g (8oz), peeled and sliced

Leeks 350g (12oz), trimmed and sliced

Potatoes 225g (8oz), peeled and sliced

Vegetable stock 750ml (1¼ pints)

Salt and freshly ground black pepper

Milk 300ml (½ pint)

Nutmeg for garnish

Flat-leaved parsley a handful, torn to garnish

1 Melt the butter in a large, lidded saucepan. Add the prepared vegetables and cook them gently for about 5 minutes.

2 Add the stock and season to taste. Bring to the boil, cover and then simmer for 30 minutes or until the vegetables are tender.

3 Transfer to a blender or food processor and purée until smooth, in batches if necessary.

4 Return the soup to the pan, add the milk and reheat gently. Serve sprinkled with freshly grated nutmeg and parsley and accompanied with warmed naan bread.

Cook's tips
•**For a mild spicy soup, stir in 1 level tbsp curry paste while cooking the vegetables in the butter.**
•**To save time (and washing up), omit the puréeing stage and serve as a chunky soup for a main course.**

Mushrooms with goat's cheese

The strong flavour of goat's cheese perfectly complements the subtlety of the mushrooms. Serve piping hot, straight from the oven.

10 minutes preparation time
30 minutes cooking time
185 Kcal per portion
12.3g fat per portion of which
7.7g is saturated
4 servings
Suitable for vegetarians

Large flat mushrooms 4, wiped

Shallots 2, peeled and finely chopped

Fresh white breadcrumbs 50g (2oz)

Lemon 1, grated rind only

Butter 25g (1oz), melted

Chopped thyme 1 tbsp, plus leaves to garnish

Salt and freshly ground black pepper

Goat's cheese 100g round cheese with rind

1 Preheat the oven to 200°C/400°F/ Gas 6. Remove the stalks from the mushrooms. Chop the stalks finely and then mix them with the shallots, breadcrumbs, lemon rind, melted butter, thyme and seasoning.

2 Divide the mixture between the mushrooms. Place the mushrooms on a baking sheet and cook them in the centre of the oven for 15 minutes, then remove from the oven.

3 Cut the cheese into 4 slices, place 1 slice on each mushroom and sprinkle over the extra thyme leaves. Return the mushrooms to the oven for a further 10–15 minutes, or until the cheese starts to melt and turn golden. Remove from the oven and serve immediately, garnished with a grinding of black pepper and accompanied with salad.

Cook's tip
•**Mushrooms don't need peeling; just wipe them over with a clean, damp cloth to remove any dirt.**

Aubergine roll-ups

A wonderfully rich combination of flavours, these can be served as a starter or snack with a few salad leaves.

10 minutes preparation time
30 minutes cooking time
410 Kcal per portion
36.5g fat per portion of which
14.8g is saturated
4 servings
Suitable for vegetarians

Aubergine 1 large

Olive oil 2–3 tbsp

Full fat cream cheese 110g (4oz)

Parmesan cheese 75g (3oz), finely grated

Pesto sauce (for home-made, see page 64), 2 tbsp

Pine nuts 50g (2oz), toasted

Sun-dried tomatoes 4, sliced

Salt and freshly ground black pepper

Extra, small whole sun-dried tomatoes in oil to garnish

Basil leaves to garnish

1 Preheat the oven to 200°C/400°F/Gas 6. Cut the ends off the aubergine and discard them. Cut the aubergine lengthways to give about 8 thin slices. Brush the oil over both sides of each slice and then cook under a hot grill for 3–4 minutes on each side, until they are a light golden colour.

2 Meanwhile, beat together the cream cheese, 50g (2oz) of the Parmesan cheese and the pesto sauce. Stir in the pine nuts, sun-dried tomatoes and season the mixture well.

3 Spread the mixture over the aubergine slices and then roll them up, secure with cocktail sticks and place in a buttered dish. Sprinkle over the remaining Parmesan cheese and bake the aubergine rolls for 10–15 minutes, or until the cheese is bubbling. Serve immediately, garnishing with sun-dried tomatoes and basil.

This is an unusual recipe for serving aubergines that blends their distinctive flavour with other Italian foods to make a delicious, attractive dish.

Cook's tip
•These may be prepared in advance up to the stage of baking them in the oven. Keep chilled for up to 24 hours and then bake just before serving. If they've been chilled, they may take a few minutes more to heat.

Tuna & caper fishcakes

These fish cakes are a great store-cupboard recipe. Use dill if you don't have any parsley and try adding a dash of Tabasco sauce.

15 minutes preparation time
30 minutes cooking time
539 Kcal per portion
32.7g fat per portion of which
16.4g is saturated
4 servings
Suitable for freezing, without sauce

Potatoes 2, peeled

Milk 2 tbsp

Tuna 400g can in oil, drained

Capers 2 tbsp, drained and chopped

Chopped parsley 2 tbsp

Salt and freshly ground black pepper

Egg 1, beaten

Fresh white breadcrumbs 50g (2oz)

Butter 50g (2oz)

For the cheese sauce:
Butter 25g (1oz)

Plain flour 25g (1oz)

Milk 300ml (½ pint)

Wholegrain mustard 1 tbsp

Salt and freshly ground black pepper

Mature Cheddar cheese 75g (3oz), grated

1 Bring a large saucepan of water to the boil. Cut the potatoes into chunks and cook in the boiling water for 12–15 minutes until they are tender, and then tip them into a colander to drain. Add the milk to the hot saucepan, return the potatoes to it and then mash until smooth. Leave to cool slightly.

2 Mix together the tuna, capers and parsley and season well. Then stir in the mashed potato. Divide the mixture into four and shape each portion into a round fishcake. Dip each fishcake into the beaten egg and then coat in the breadcrumbs.

3 Heat the butter in a frying pan and cook the fishcakes for 4–5 minutes on each side until lightly golden.

4 To make the sauce, heat the butter in a saucepan until melted and then add the flour. Cook over a medium heat for 1–2 minutes until the flour thickens into a paste. Gradually add the milk, bringing the mixture to the boil between each addition, and beating well to give a smooth sauce.

5 Stir in the mustard and seasoning and simmer for a couple of minutes. Remove the pan from the heat and add the cheese. Stir the sauce until the cheese melts, returning the pan briefly to the heat, if necessary, to encourage the cheese to melt.

6 Serve the fishcakes on individual plates with the sauce poured alongside and accompanied by mixed green salad leaves.

Cook's tips
•Place the fishcakes on a sheet of baking parchment in a freezer-proof container and cover and freeze for up to 1 month. Allow the fishcakes to defrost in the fridge overnight before cooking.
•Chilling the fishcakes before cooking them will make them firmer and less likely to break apart during cooking.

Smoked salmon mousse

These mousses look impressive as a starter for a special meal or are good served with toast for a supper dish. They keep in the fridge for up to 3 days.

10 minutes preparation time
1 hour minimum chilling time
377 Kcal per portion
29.2g fat per portion of which
15.8g is saturated
4 servings
Suitable for freezing

Smoked salmon 300g (11oz) or about 8 slices

Cream cheese 200g carton

Tartar sauce 2 tbsp

Chopped dill 1 tbsp, plus sprigs to garnish

Salt and freshly ground black pepper

Tabasco sauce a dash

Large cooked prawns 110g (4oz)

1 Use one slice of smoked salmon to line the edge of each hole in a four-holed muffin tin, cutting the slice in half if necessary.

2 Finely chop the remaining salmon and mix it into the cream cheese, together with the tartar sauce, dill, seasoning and Tabasco sauce to taste. Reserve 8 prawns for garnishing and carefully stir the rest into the cream cheese mixture.

3 Divide the mixture between the lined muffin tin holes. Level the surface with a knife and cover with cling film. Chill for at least 1 hour before serving.

4 To serve, carefully lift the mousses out of the tin and peel away the cling film. Invert each mousse onto individual serving plates and then decorate them with two prawns and a sprig of dill.

Cook's tips
•Wrap the mousses well and freeze for up to 1 month.
•Smoked trout may be used instead of smoked salmon, or for another variation make the filling using hot smoked or poached salmon.

Hot turkey salad

This is a great way of using up leftover turkey. You can also use any meat to make up the weight given for the turkey – turkey and ham is a good combo.

10 minutes preparation time
15–20 minutes cooking time
305 Kcal per portion
16.6g fat per portion of which
7.5g is saturated
4 servings

Butter 25g (1oz)

Onion 1, peeled and cut into thin wedges

Button mushrooms 110g (4oz), wiped

Smoked streaky bacon 6 rashers

Cooked turkey 350g (12oz), diced

Red wine vinegar 2 tbsp

Sherry 3 tbsp

Salt and freshly ground black pepper

Water or baby spinach leaves 75–150g packet

1 Heat the butter in a frying pan and fry the onion for 3–4 minutes until it starts to soften. Add the mushrooms and cook for a further 3–4 minutes until they start to crisp. Remove from the pan and leave on one side.

2 Cut the bacon rashers in half and roll them up. Add the bacon rolls to the pan and cook for 3–4 minutes until starting to brown, then add the turkey and cook for a further 2–3 minutes or until heated through. Stir in the vinegar, sherry and seasoning, then return the onion and mushrooms to the pan.

3 Arrange the spinach leaves on individual plates and spoon the turkey mixture on top. Spoon over the juices from the pan to warm the leaves slightly and serve immediately.

Cook's tip
•**If you like wilted leaves, stir the spinach into the hot pan with the turkey mixture just before serving.**

Vegetable stroganoff

This creamy-tasting stroganoff is much lower in fat than you would imagine as it's made with yogurt.

10 minutes preparation time
35 minutes cooking time
311 Kcal per portion
14.3g fat per portion of which
6.6g is saturated
4 servings
Suitable for vegetarians

Red split lentils 75g (3oz)

Butter 25g (1oz)

Carrots 2, peeled and sliced

Onions 225g (8oz), peeled and sliced

Garlic 1 clove, peeled and crushed

Green pepper 110g (4oz), deseeded and sliced

Red pepper 110g (4oz), deseeded and sliced

Tomatoes 2, skinned (see Cook's Tip) and chopped

Salt and freshly ground black pepper

Dessert apples 2, peeled, cored and diced

Dried sage 1 tsp

Mixed peanuts and raisins 3 tbsp

Full fat soft cheese 50g (2oz)

Low fat natural yogurt 200g (7oz)

Cook's tip

• **To remove the tomato skins, make a long cut in the skin, soak in boiling water for 5 minutes and then transfer to a bowl of cold water.**

1 Cook the lentils in 200ml (7fl oz) water for 5–10 minutes, until just tender. Boil off any excess liquid.

2 Heat the butter in a large, lidded frying pan. Add the carrots, cover and sauté for 10 minutes. Add the onions, garlic, peppers and tomatoes, season generously and cook for 10 minutes, stirring occasionally.

3 Add the apples and sage and cook for a further 5 minutes. Stir in the lentils, peanuts and raisins. Blend the soft cheese with the yogurt and then stir into the vegetables. Reheat gently and serve with crusty French bread.

Broccoli & Stilton lasagne

This is a vegetarian version of the much-loved Italian lasagne and is delicious served with garlic bread.

15 minutes preparation time
50–60 minutes cooking time
582 Kcal per portion
31.7g fat per portion of which
18.3g is saturated
4–6 servings
Suitable for freezing
Suitable for vegetarians

Broccoli 750g (1lb 10oz), cut into florets

Red peppers 2, deseeded and sliced

Courgettes 2, trimmed and sliced

Lasagne 6–8 sheets

Nutmeg freshly grated

Parmesan cheese freshly grated, 1–2 tbsp

For the cheese sauce:
Butter 50g (2oz)

Plain flour 50g (2oz)

Milk 600ml (1 pint)

Stilton cheese 175g (6oz), crumbled

Salt and freshly ground black pepper

Cook's tip

•**To freeze, prepare the lasagne in a freezer-proof dish, up to the stage that it's ready to go in the oven. Cover and freeze for up to 1 month. Allow it to defrost in the fridge overnight before baking it. It may need a little longer in the oven as it is being cooked from chilled.**

1 Preheat the oven to 200°C/400°F/Gas 6. Bring a large saucepan of water to the boil and add the broccoli. Cook for 2 minutes, then add the red peppers and courgettes to the saucepan, bring to the boil again and cook for a further 2 minutes.

2 Drain and rinse the vegetables under cold running water to cool them down quickly.

3 To make the cheese sauce, melt the butter in a saucepan, add the flour and cook for 1–2 minutes, stirring well. Gradually add the milk, beating well and allowing it to come to the boil between each addition of liquid to give a smooth sauce. Add the Stilton and stir until it melts and then remove the pan from the heat. Season the sauce to taste.

4 Spoon half of the vegetables into a lasagne dish and top with just less than one-third of the cheese sauce. Cover with a layer of lasagne. Spoon the remaining vegetables on top and spread over just less than half of the remaining cheese sauce, then cover with another layer of lasagne. Spoon the remaining sauce on top and smooth out. Grate some nutmeg over the top and then sprinkle over the Parmesan cheese.

5 Bake the lasagne for 40–50 minutes, until it's bubbling and the top is golden brown. If it starts to brown too quickly, cover it with a sheet of foil. Serve immediately.

Creamy vegetable crumble

This is substantial enough to be served as a vegetarian main meal with ciabatta bread, or may be served as a side dish to accompany grilled chops or sausages.

10 minutes preparation time
45 minutes cooking time
542 Kcal per portion
27.1g fat per portion of which
15g is saturated
4 servings
Suitable for vegetarians

Water 1 litre (1¾ pints)

Vegetable stock cubes 2

Sweet potatoes 2, peeled and cut into chunks

Carrots 2, peeled and cut into chunks

Parsnips 2, peeled and cut into chunks

Leeks 2, washed and cut into thick slices

Sweetcorn kernels 198g can, drained

Cornflour 1 tbsp, optional

Soft goat's cheese with black pepper or chives 110g packet

Salt and freshly ground black pepper

For the crumble topping:
Plain flour 110g (4oz)

Butter 50g (2oz), cubed

Mature Cheddar cheese 110g (4oz), grated

Cook's tip
•**Try using different cheeses as variations – a soft cheese with garlic and herbs is good in the sauce, and Stilton works well in the topping in place of the Cheddar.**

1 Preheat the oven to 220°C/425°F/ Gas 7. Pour the water into a large, lidded saucepan and bring it to the boil. Crumble in the stock cubes and stir until they have dissolved.

2 Add the sweet potato and carrot chunks. Bring the pan to the boil, then cover, reduce the heat and allow to simmer for 5 minutes. Add the parsnips and leeks.

3 Re-cover the pan and bring it back to the boil, then simmer for 10–15 minutes until the vegetables are just tender. Using a draining spoon, transfer the vegetables to an ovenproof dish, reserving the cooking liquor. Scatter the sweetcorn over the top of the vegetables.

4 Bring the cooking liquid to a rapid boil, uncovered, and boil to reduce the quantity by about half. If necessary, thicken with cornflour. Remove the pan from the heat and crumble in the goat's cheese. Stir until the cheese melts, to form a sauce. Add seasoning to taste and pour the sauce over the vegetables in the dish.

5 To make the crumble topping, sift the flour into a bowl, add the cubed butter and rub it in to form coarse breadcrumbs, then stir in the cheese. Sprinkle this crumble mixture over the vegetables and bake for 20–25 minutes until the topping is golden and the sauce is bubbling. Serve the dish immediately.

Savoury crumble is always a treat. For a more crunchy mixture, use rolled oats instead of half of the flour. You could also add nuts to the topping.

Smoked fish bake

Here is a fish pie that is perfect for a light lunch or supper. For the best flavour, use natural smoked fish rather than artificially dyed yellow haddock.

10 minutes preparation time
20 minutes cooking time
520 Kcal per portion
21.3g fat per portion of which
10.1g is saturated
4 servings

Butter 60g (2½oz), melted

Plain flour 40g (1½oz)

Milk 450ml (¾ pint)

Smoked haddock 450g (1lb), skinned and cubed

Frozen peas 75g (3oz)

Sweetcorn kernels ½ x 198g can, drained

Salt and freshly ground black pepper

Chopped parsley 1 tbsp

Lemon ½, grated rind and juice

Filo pastry 4 sheets

Sesame seeds 2 tbsp

Cook's tip
•**Keep the filo pastry well wrapped when you're not handling it as it dries out very quickly, and if this happens it will crumble rather than scrunch up for the top.**

1 Preheat the oven to 190°C/375°F/ Gas 5. Melt 40g (1½oz) of the butter in a saucepan, add the flour and beat to form a paste. Gradually add the milk, bringing the mixture to the boil between each addition of liquid. Once all the milk has been added, simmer the white sauce gently for 2–3 minutes to ensure the flour is cooked through.

2 Add the haddock, peas and sweetcorn to the sauce and cook for 5 minutes. Season and add the parsley, lemon rind and juice. Transfer to a shallow, ovenproof dish.

3 Divide each sheet of filo into three and brush one side with melted butter. Scrunch up the pastry and lay on top of the fish mixture. Sprinkle with sesame seeds and bake for 20 minutes, until golden. Serve with a baked potato and purple sprouting broccoli.

Salmon & fennel en croute

This recipe looks really impressive but is actually very simple to make.
It is perfect for dinner with friends.

15 minutes preparation time
50 minutes cooking time
523 Kcal per portion
30.6g fat per portion of which
9.7g is saturated
4 servings

Salmon fillet 450g (1lb)

Lemon ½, grated rind and juice

Fennel 1 bulb, trimmed and roughly chopped

White bread 2 slices, crusts removed

Chopped dill 3 tbsp

Salt and freshly ground black pepper

Puff pastry 250–350g (9–12oz)

Parma ham 4 slices

Egg 1 yolk

1 Preheat the oven to 220°C/425°F/ Gas 7. Check there aren't any bones in the salmon fillet and then squeeze over the lemon juice.

2 Put the fennel and bread in a food processor and whizz until finely chopped. Tip the mixture into a bowl and add the dill and lemon rind and season well.

3 Roll out the pastry to about 25cm (10in) wide and 5cm (2in) longer than the length of the salmon. Cut the pastry in half. Put one strip on a greased baking sheet and prick it over with a fork. Lay the slices of ham on top, placing them across the pastry so they hang over the edges.

4 Place the fennel mixture down the centre of the ham-lined pastry, leaving a 2.5cm (1in) rim around the edge. Place the salmon on top and bring the ham ends up over it to enclose it. Roll out the other pastry strip so it is slightly larger than the first.

5 Brush around the pastry rim with water and place the strip over the salmon. Press the edges well to seal them. Trim the edges straight and then use a knife to scallop the edge. Lightly beat the egg yolk with 1 tbsp water and brush over the pastry.

6 Bake the salmon in the centre of the oven for 20 minutes, then turn down the temperature to 190°C/ 375°F/Gas 5, and bake for a further 20–30 minutes. Remove the salmon from the oven and leave it to 'rest' in a warm place for about 5 minutes so it is easier to slice.

Cook's tip
•This dish can be made up to 4 hours in advance without the glaze and kept chilled. Glaze it just before cooking. To save time, use ready-rolled puff pastry.

Turkey with sherry gravy

For a really festive meal, treat your guests to this turkey recipe on Christmas Day. The lemon, parsley and thyme stuffing is good to eat cold, too.

15 minutes preparation time
4½–4¾ hours cooking time plus resting
714 Kcal per portion
35.4g fat per portion of which
17.9g is saturated
6 servings with plenty left for eating cold

For the stuffing:
Fresh white breadcrumbs 250g (9oz)
Chopped parsley 6–8 tbsp
Chopped thyme 1–2 tbsp
Lemon 1, grated rind
Butter 110g (4oz), melted
Egg 1
Salt and freshly ground black pepper

For the turkey:
Turkey 5–6kg (11–13lb)
Turkey or chicken stock 600ml (1 pint)
Butter 50g (2oz), softened
Herbs to garnish

For the gravy:
Plain flour 3 tbsp
Gravy browning optional
Sherry 2 tbsp

Rosemary leaves to garnish
Lemon thyme leaves to garnish

1 Preheat the oven to 190°C/375°F/ Gas 5. To make the stuffing, place all the ingredients in a large bowl and mix together, taking care not to press it together too much – it should remain light and open in texture.

2 To prepare the turkey, rinse out the inside and pat dry. Press the stuffing into the neck cavity, shaping any extra stuffing into balls, which can be cooked on a small baking tray at the top of the oven for 15–20 minutes.

3 Pull the neck skin over the stuffing and secure with a skewer or a couple of wooden cocktail sticks. Weigh the turkey to calculate the cooking time, allowing 20 minutes per 450g (1lb). A turkey with stuffing that weighs about 6kg (13lb) will take approximately 4½–4¾ hours to cook.

4 Place the turkey in a roasting tin, pour the stock around it and spread the softened butter over the skin. Cover with foil and place towards the bottom of the oven (the shelf above the turkey at the top of the oven can be used for roasting vegetables).

5 Keep the turkey covered with foil until the last 45 minutes of the calculated cooking time, then remove foil, baste and return to the oven until cooked through.

6 To test if the turkey is cooked, pierce the thickest part of the flesh of the thigh with a skewer – if the juices that run out are clear, it's cooked, but if the juices are still pink, then the bird needs further cooking. When cooked, remove it from the oven, and transfer to a warmed serving plate. Cover the turkey with clean foil and leave it to 'rest' in a warm place for 20–30 minutes as this will make carving easier.

7 To make the gravy, pour the juices from the roasting tin into a fat separator or jug. Return 3 tbsp of the fat to the roasting tin and skim as much fat as possible off the rest of the juices and discard it.

8 Place the roasting tin on the hob and stir in the flour for the gravy. Cook over a gentle heat for a couple of minutes, then slowly stir in skimmed turkey juices. Bring to the boil and, if it is too thick, then stir in some boiling water to give the desired consistency and add a little gravy browning if liked. Stir in the sherry and season to taste. Keep piping hot until serving and pour into a warmed gravy boat.

9 Serve the turkey garnished with rosemary and lemon thyme and accompanied with stuffing balls, roast potatoes, steamed vegetables, and orange halves stuffed with lightly cooked cranberries.

Chicken & apple casserole

This wholesome casserole is delicious served with a double mash of potato and parsnip together with some steamed leaks to add yet more flavour.

15 minutes preparation time
1 hour 20 minutes cooking time
664 Kcal per portion
45.7g fat per portion of which
10.7g is saturated
4 servings
Suitable for freezing

Butter 25g (1oz)

Vegetable oil 1 tbsp

Salt and freshly ground black pepper

Chicken quarters 4, skin left on

Dessert apples 2, peeled, cored and cut into thick wedges

Chopped thyme 1–2 tbsp

Onion 1, peeled and sliced

Smoked bacon pieces 110g (4oz)

Plain flour 2 tbsp

Dry cider 300ml (½ pint)

Chicken stock 150ml (¼ pint)

Double cream 4 tbsp

Cook's tips

• **Use crisp dessert apples in this recipe as cooking apples will turn to pulp.**
• **Spoon the cold mixture into a freezer-proof container, cover and freeze for up to 1 month. Allow to defrost overnight before reheating thoroughly.**

1 Preheat the oven to 200°C/400°F/Gas 6. Melt the butter in a frying pan and add the oil. Season the chicken and add to the pan.

2 Cook for 6–7 minutes, turning occasionally, to brown the surface. Remove from the pan and place in a lidded casserole dish. Add the apple on top and sprinkle over the thyme.

3 Add the onion to the frying pan and cook for 5–6 minutes until it starts to soften. Add the bacon pieces and continue to cook for a further 4–5 minutes. Transfer the onion and bacon to the casserole dish.

4 Add the flour to the juices in the pan and stir until they form a thick paste, then slowly add the cider and stock, stirring well and bringing the mixture to the boil after each addition of liquid. Pour over the chicken in the casserole dish and cover.

5 Cook in the centre of the oven for 50–60 minutes, or until the juices run clear when the chicken is pierced with a skewer. Stir in the cream just before serving and season to taste.

Lamb stew with herb dumplings

This is a traditional favourite 'comfort' food – just remember to simmer it gently. The old saying is: 'A stew boiled is a stew spoiled.'

15 minutes preparation time
1½–1¾ hours cooking time
721 Kcal per portion
41.9g fat per portion of which
19.8g is saturated
4 servings
Suitable for freezing without the dumplings

For the stew:

Butter 50g (2oz)

Vegetable oil 1 tbsp

Lamb 350g (12oz) diced leg

Onion 1, peeled and cut into thin wedges

Potatoes 2 red-skinned, cut into chunks

Carrots 2, peeled and cut into chunks

Parsnip 2, peeled and cut into chunks

Swede ½, peeled and cut into chunks

Plain flour 2 tbsp

Water 600ml (1 pint)

Lamb stock cube 1

Worcestershire sauce a dash

Salt and freshly ground black pepper

For the dumplings:

Self-raising flour 150g (5oz)

Shredded suet 75g (3oz), vegetable or beef

Chopped rosemary 2 tbsp, plus a few leaves to garnish

1 Heat half the butter and the oil in a large, lidded frying pan and add the lamb. Cook the meat for 5–8 minutes, turning the meat occasionally until it's browned on all surfaces, then remove it from the pan.

2 Add the remaining butter to the pan and heat until it's bubbling, then add the onion and vegetables and cook for 4–5 minutes. Stir in the flour and cook the stew for 1–2 minutes, then gradually stir in the water, bringing the pan's contents to the boil between each addition to make a smooth gravy.

3 Crumble in the stock cube and stir until dissolved. Return the meat to the pan. Bring the stew to a gentle simmer, cover and simmer gently for 1 hour. Stir in the Worcestershire sauce and seasoning to taste.

4 To make the dumplings, sift the flour into a bowl. Stir in the suet, rosemary and seasoning and add enough water to make a soft dough. Divide the dough into four, shape it into balls and place on top of the stew. Cover the pan and simmer for about 20 minutes, until the dumplings have risen. Serve immediately with a few extra rosemary leaves snipped over the dumplings.

Cook's tip

•The dumplings are not suitable for freezing, but the lamb stew may be packed into a freezer-proof container when it's cold and then frozen for up to 1 month. Allow it to defrost in the fridge overnight before reheating thoroughly and adding dumplings.

Sausage & leek supper

This is the perfect dish for a wintery evening. It could be a warming and comforting treat after a long day Christmas shopping.

20 minutes preparation time
45 minutes cooking time
480 Kcal per portion
26.8g fat per portion of which
12.2g is saturated
6 servings
Suitable for freezing

Potatoes 680g (1½lb), peeled and sliced

Butter 25g (1oz)

Vegetable oil 2 tsp

Pork sausages with herbs 450g (1lb), sliced

Onion 1, peeled and sliced

Leeks 4, washed, trimmed and sliced

Plain flour 40g (1½oz)

Milk 450ml (16fl oz)

Smoked Cheddar cheese (Applewood) 110g (4oz), grated

Fresh breadcrumbs 25g (1oz)

1 Preheat the oven to 180°C/350°F/ Gas 4. Bring a large saucepan of lightly salted water to the boil. Add the potatoes and cook for 5–10 minutes. Drain the potatoes and wipe out the saucepan.

2 Melt the butter in the saucepan, add the oil and sausages and cook for 5 minutes, until browned all over.

3 Add the onion and leeks and cook for a further 5 minutes, until softened. Then add the flour, cook for 1 minute and gradually add the milk.

4 Heat, stirring continuously, until the sauce thickens, and becomes smooth. Cook for 1 minute.

5 Remove the saucepan from the heat, add 75g (3oz) of the cheese and stir until melted. Transfer to an ovenproof dish, arrange the potato slices on top and sprinkle with the remaining cheese and breadcrumbs.

6 Bake the dish in the oven for 35–45 minutes until the topping is browned. Serve with steamed carrots and cabbage.

Sausage and leek is a great combination. Add interest by using two contrasting varieties of sausage, or even some of the spicier chorizo.

Cook's tip
•If you are unable to obtain Applewood Cheddar, simply use an unsmoked mature Cheddar cheese.

Sausage cassoulet

This is a quick version of the traditional French cassoulet. The combination of pork and tomato flavours works very well with the crunchy topping.

15 minutes preparation time
1½ hours cooking time
614 Kcal per portion
39.8g fat per portion of which
17.1g is saturated
4 servings

Butter 25g (1oz)

Lincolnshire sausages 450g (1lb)

Onion 1, peeled and sliced

Smoked streaky bacon 6 rashers, chopped

Chopped tomatoes 400g can

Baked beans 425g can

Pork or ham stock cube 1, crumbled

Salt and freshly ground black pepper

For the topping:
Fresh white breadcrumbs 50g (2oz)

Butter 25g (1oz), melted

Garlic 1 clove, peeled and crushed

Chopped parsley 1 tbsp

1 Preheat the oven to 180°C/350°F/ Gas 4. Melt the butter in a frying pan, add the sausages and cook over a medium heat until they have browned. Remove from the pan and place them in a casserole dish.

2 Add the onion and bacon to the pan and cook for 5–7 minutes, until the onion starts to soften.

3 Stir in the tomatoes, baked beans and stock cube and return the sausages to the pan. Season to taste, taking care not to add too much salt if the bacon is salty. Pour the mixture into a casserole dish.

4 To make the topping, tip the breadcrumbs into a bowl and stir in the butter, garlic and parsley. Sprinkle the topping over the sausages and then bake in the centre of the oven for 50 minutes–1 hour, until the topping is golden in colour. Serve the cassoulet with a fresh green salad with mustard dressing.

Cook's tip
•**Try to use good-quality sausages as cheaper ones can make the dish taste greasy.**

Marinated pork with pepper

This colourful dish looks great served with plain white rice or, for a variation, serve with buttered egg noodles.

10 minutes preparation time plus marinating
25 minutes cooking time
251 Kcal per portion
10.3g fat per portion of which
4.8g is saturated
4 servings
Suitable for freezing

Soy sauce 2 tbsp

Worcestershire sauce 1 tbsp

Tomato ketchup 4 tbsp

Clear honey 1 tbsp

English mustard 1 tsp

Pork fillet 450g (1lb), sliced

Butter 25g (1oz)

Onion 1, peeled and chopped

Vegetable stock 150ml (¼ pint)

Red or green pepper 1, deseeded and sliced

Mushrooms 75g (3oz), wiped and sliced

Cook's tips
•Diced pork can be used, but it may need to be simmered for a little longer to tenderise it as it isn't as tender as pork fillet, although it is cheaper to buy.
•For a spicy dish, use sweet chilli dipping sauce in place of the tomato ketchup.

1 In a bowl, mix together the sauces, ketchup, honey and mustard. Add the pork and then leave to marinate for 30 minutes.

2 Melt the butter in a large, lidded frying pan and cook the onion and pork (reserving the marinade), until they have browned.

3 Add the stock and marinade, then cover and simmer for 20 minutes, until the pork is cooked.

4 Add the pepper and mushrooms and cook for a further 3 minutes or until the sauce has reduced to a coating consistency. Serve on a bed of basmati rice.

Pork & apricot casserole

An ideal dish to make after a busy day. It's quick to prepare and once it's in the oven, you can forget about it.

10 minutes preparation time
1¾–2 hours cooking time
570 Kcal per portion
32.9g fat per portion of which
12.9g is saturated
4 servings
Suitable for freezing

Butter 25g (1oz)

Vegetable oil 1 tbsp

Pork loin steaks 4

Carrots 2, peeled and thickly sliced

Shallots 8, peeled

Root ginger 2.5cm (1in), peeled and grated

Plain flour 2 tbsp

Cider 440ml can

Dried ready-to-eat apricots 175g (6oz)

Salt and freshly ground black pepper

Wholegrain mustard 1 tbsp

1 Preheat the oven to 180°C/350°F/Gas 4. Heat half the butter and all the oil in a frying pan and add the pork to brown it well on both sides, then remove it from the pan.

2 Add the remaining butter to the pan and then the carrots, shallots and ginger, and cook for 2–3 minutes. Stir in the flour and then the cider and bring to the boil, stirring well, until the sauce thickens.

3 Return the pork to the pan, stir in the apricots and season to taste. Transfer the mixture to a lidded casserole dish, cover and cook in the centre of the oven for 1½–1¾ hours, or until the meat is tender. Remove from the oven and stir in the mustard.

4 Serve the casserole on a bed of couscous flecked with chopped parsley and mixed with a little olive oil and lemon juice.

Using wholegrain mustard adds bite to this dish and balances the sweetness of the apricots. It adds visual interest, too.

Cook's tips
• Use dried ready-to-eat prunes as an alternative to the apricots.
• Pack into a freezer-proof container and seal and freeze for up to 1 month. Allow to defrost before reheating in a saucepan over a moderate heat until boiling and completely cooked through.

Bacon, tomato & walnut pasta

This dish has an unusual texture owing to the addition of crunchy walnuts and breadcrumbs. Serve it immediately so the breadcrumbs don't soften.

5 minutes preparation time
20 minutes cooking time
748 Kcal per portion
38.6g fat per portion of which
11.8g is saturated
4 servings

Pasta 350g (12oz), penne or spirals

Tomatoes 8, preferably plum, halved

Olive oil 4 tbsp

Light muscovado sugar 1 tbsp

Salt and freshly ground black pepper

Butter 50g (2oz)

Smoked bacon bits 110g (4oz)

Roughly chopped walnuts 50g (2oz)

Fresh white breadcrumbs 50g (2oz)

Garlic 1 clove, peeled and crushed

Chopped basil 2 tbsp

1 Cook the pasta in boiling salted water for 10–12 minutes, or as directed on the packet, and then drain well.

2 Meanwhile, place the tomato halves on a grill pan, cut side up, brush with 2 tbsp of the olive oil, sprinkle over the sugar and season with salt and freshly ground black pepper. Cook under a hot grill for 5–8 minutes, or until the tomatoes start to char, then remove from the grill and keep warm until the pasta is cooked.

3 Heat half the butter in a frying pan and add the bacon bits. Cook them over a medium heat for 5–7 minutes until they start to crisp, then remove them from the pan.

4 Add the remaining butter to the pan, tip in the walnuts, breadcrumbs and garlic, and cook over a moderate heat until the breadcrumbs turn golden. Remove the pan from the heat and stir in the basil and bacon bits and then season with salt (if needed) and pepper.

5 Pour the remaining oil over the pasta and then stir in the bacon, tomato and walnut mixture. Serve immediately.

Bacon is a great partner for pasta (see also the Mexican-style pasta on page 86), but as it can be very salty, be sure to taste a cooked piece before you add the seasoning.

Cook's tip
•**For a vegetarian version, leave out the bacon bits and stir in a few rocket or baby spinach leaves at the end of cooking so they wilt into the pasta.**

Peppered steaks & mushrooms

Steak and chips is always a winner, and this recipe is no exception. The mushroom and Madeira sauce makes it particularly special.

5 minutes preparation time
25 minutes cooking time
533 Kcal per portion
35.9g fat per portion of which
18.8g is saturated
4 servings

Peppercorns 1 tbsp, coarsely crushed

Steak 4 fillet or rump

Water 150ml (¼ pint), boiling

Dried mushrooms 15g (½oz)

Butter 25g (1oz)

Vegetable oil 1 tbsp

Button mushrooms 110g (4oz), wiped and sliced

Madeira 6 tbsp

Double cream 142ml carton

Salt and freshly ground black pepper

1 Press the peppercorns onto both sides of the steaks. Pour the boiling water over the dried mushrooms and leave them to soak for about 10 minutes.

2 Heat the butter and oil in a frying pan until hot and then add the steaks to the pan and cook for 2–3 minutes on each side. Remove them from the pan and keep warm.

3 Add the button mushrooms to the pan and cook for 3–5 minutes, stirring occasionally, until they start to turn golden. Add the soaked dried mushrooms together with their liquid and then add the Madeira.

4 Simmer the mixture gently for 1–2 minutes to soften the dried mushrooms, then boil rapidly to reduce the liquid by about half. Pour the cream into the pan and return the steaks to the pan.

5 Cover and simmer gently for 5–10 minutes, until the steaks are cooked through to the desired level of pinkness. Remove the steaks from the pan and, if the sauce is too thin, boil it rapidly to reduce it to the desired thickness. Season it to taste and spoon over the steaks. Serve immediately with chips and a mixed leaf salad.

Cook's tip

•**This recipe also works well with chicken breast in place of the steak – just allow a little extra cooking time to ensure the chicken is thoroughly cooked through.**

Steak & kidney pudding

Traditional British food at its best. The pudding takes a while to steam, but is well worth the wait.

10 minutes preparation time
2½–3 hours cooking time
669 Kcal per portion
35g fat per portion of which
15.4g is saturated
4 servings

For the filling:
Rump steak 350g (12oz), cubed

Lambs' kidneys 2–3, cored and chopped

Onion 1, peeled and chopped

Button mushrooms 110g (4oz), wiped

Plain flour 2 tbsp

Chopped thyme 1 tbsp

Salt and freshly ground black pepper

Water 150ml (¼ pint) boiling

Beef stock cube 1

For the suet pastry:
Self-raising flour 250g (8oz)

Beef suet 110g (4oz)

Salt and freshly ground black pepper

Cook's tip
•**As an alternative to the beef, try using diced chicken breast, and 3–4 rashers smoked bacon, cut into pieces, in place of the kidneys. Replace the stock cube with a chicken one.**

1 Place the steak, kidneys, onion, mushrooms, flour, thyme and seasoning into a bowl and mix together so the meat and vegetables are coated in the flour. Pour the water over the stock cube and leave it to cool slightly.

2 To make the pastry, mix together the flour, suet and seasoning in a large bowl. Add sufficient cold water to the mix to give a soft but workable dough. Then lightly knead the pastry to make a ball.

3 Roll the pastry out on a lightly floured surface to a round large enough to line a 1.25 litre (2 pint) pudding basin, plus 2.5cm (1in) extra all around. Cut out a quarter wedge from the circle and set this piece aside for the top.

4 Lightly butter the basin and then line it with the pastry with the wedge cut out, overlapping the cut edges to make a seal and bringing the pastry up the sides so it comes above the top rim by about 1cm (½in). Fill the lined bowl with the meat mixture and pour over the stock.

5 Gather the reserved piece of pastry into a ball and roll it out to a round that just fits in the top of the basin. Moisten the edge of the pastry around the rim of the bowl and place the circular piece on top. Pinch together the edges and then pull the outside edge over onto the top of the pudding to make an extra good seal prior to steaming.

6 Cover with a piece of baking parchment with a pleat in it to allow for expansion of the pudding during steaming, and then cover tightly with a sheet of foil. Put the basin in a steamer or on a trivet in a large pan. Fill the pan to at least halfway up the bowl with boiling water and then cover with a well-fitting lid and steam for 2½–3 hours. Check the water level about every half hour to ensure the pan does not boil dry, and, if necessary, top up the level with hot water from a kettle.

7 When cooked, take the pudding out of the steamer and leave it to rest for 10–15 minutes. Turn out onto a large warmed plate – with a lip because the gravy may pour out when you cut it – and serve immediately with steamed green vegetables such as broccoli or cabbage.

Fruity coffee pancakes

This dessert is wonderfully light and fruity and so works well after a heavy main course. If you make the batter in advance, it is quick to cook, too.

15 minutes preparation time
20 minutes cooking time
305 Kcal per portion
8.3g fat per portion of which
4.5g is saturated
4 servings
Suitable for vegetarians

Plain flour 110g (4oz)

Instant coffee granules
1 tsp

Egg 1, beaten

Milk 300ml (½ pint)

Butter 25g (1oz)

Oranges 2

Cornflour 2 tsp

Clear honey 2 tbsp

Bananas 2, peeled and chopped

Greek-style natural yogurt to serve

1 Place the flour and coffee granules in a mixing bowl and gradually stir in the egg and then the milk to form a smooth batter.

2 Heat a little butter of the in a frying pan. When hot, pour in 3 tbsp of the batter, tilting the pan to cover the base. Cook the batter until the pancake moves freely, then flip it over and cook until the other side is golden. Repeat to make 8 pancakes, keeping them warm while making the filling.

3 Remove the rind from the oranges with a zester. Using a small, sharp knife, take away as much of the pith as possible. Holding each orange over a bowl, slice in between each segment to release the flesh and juice into the bowl. Mix the orange juice, cornflour and honey and heat in a small pan until thickened. Add the fruit.

4 Fold the pancakes into triangles and fill with the fruit. Serve immediately with the Greek yogurt.

Cook's tips
•**Use a heavy frying pan with a diameter of up to 18cm (7in) – the batter won't spread as evenly in a larger one.**
•**Use only a little fat (butter is best), but re-grease after cooking each pancake.**

Dried fruit compote

This tangy dish is ideal for a light dessert or even for breakfast. It's quick to make but needs a long time to soak.

5 minutes preparation time plus soaking
2 minutes cooking time
164 Kcal per portion
0.5g fat per portion of which
0.2g is saturated
4 servings
Suitable for vegetarians

Lemonade 300ml (½ pint)
Cloves 6
Cinnamon sticks 2 x 6cm (2½in)
Orange 1, zested rind
Dried fruit salad 250g packet
Orange juice 150ml (¼ pint)

Cook's tip
•**Dried fruit salad is a mixture of dried fruits that usually contains apples, prunes, peaches and pears. If you're unable to find it ready mixed, then make your own mixture.**

1 Warm the lemonade gently in a lidded saucepan so that it loses its fizz. Bring it to the boil and pour into a large bowl. Stir in the cloves, cinnamon, orange rind and the dried fruit salad. Leave the mixture for at least 4 hours, or overnight, for the fruit to pulp up.

2 Using a small, sharp knife, take away as much of the pith as possible from the zested orange. Holding the orange over a bowl, slice in between each segment to release the flesh and juice into the bowl. Stir the orange segments and juice into the compote and warm through before serving.

Chocolate & Irish cream roulade

This indulgent roulade is best eaten on the day that it's made, but will keep for up to 2 days in the fridge.

15 minutes preparation time
25 minutes cooking time plus chilling
649 Kcal per portion
40.8g fat per portion of which
22.2g is saturated
6–8 servings
Suitable for vegetarians

For the roulade:
Eggs 5 large, separated
Caster sugar 175g (6oz)
Plain chocolate 175g (6oz), melted, plus 1 small bar to decorate

For the filling:
Double cream 300ml (½ pint)
Icing sugar 2 tbsp, plus extra for dusting
Irish cream liqueur 4–6 tbsp

1 Preheat the oven to 180°C/350°F/ Gas 4. Whisk the egg whites until stiff. Place the egg yolks and sugar in a separate bowl and whisk them together until the mixture leaves a trail when the whisk is lifted up. Fold the chocolate into the egg yolk mixture then fold in the egg whites.

2 Pour the mixture into a 33 x 23cm (13 x 9in) Swiss roll tin, lined with baking parchment. Use a palette knife to spread the mixture out to the edges, taking care not to knock out too much of the air.

3 Bake the roulade in the centre of the oven for 20–25 minutes, or until the mixture has just set in the centre. Remove from the oven, leave it in the tin and cover with a clean, damp tea towel. Leave the roulade to cool for at least 4 hours or overnight.

4 To make the filling, whip the cream until it forms soft peaks, then fold in the icing sugar and Irish cream liqueur to taste. Dust a sheet of baking parchment with icing sugar and turn the roulade out onto it. Peel away the lining paper from the roulade and spread over the cream. Roll up using the paper to help. Keep the roulade chilled until ready to serve.

5 Use a swivel-bladed vegetable peeler to make the chocolate curls. If the chocolate doesn't curl easily, warm the block in a microwave in 20-second bursts on full power until curls form easily when the peeler blade is used. Before serving, dust the roulade with a little extra icing sugar and scatter over the curls.

Pure indulgence! This roulade might keep for 2 days, but you are unlikely to have to put that claim to the test!

Cook's tip
•**Whisking the egg whites for the roulade first means you can use the same beaters for the egg yolk mixture, which saves washing them.**

Cranberry & apple tarte tatin

Serve this dessert as an alternative to Christmas pudding. The addition of the dried cranberries contrasts wonderfully with the sweet caramel.

15 minutes preparation time
40 minutes cooking time
570 Kcal per portion
28.8g fat per portion of which
17.7g is saturated
6–8 servings
Suitable for vegetarians

For the pastry:
Plain flour 250g (9oz)
Butter 150g (5oz), cubed
Icing sugar 50g (2oz)
Egg 1

For the topping:
Butter 50g (2oz)
Caster sugar 110g (4oz)
Water 2 tbsp
Dried cranberries 50g (2oz)
Dessert apples
500–750g (1–1½lb), peeled, cored and sliced

Cream for serving

1 Preheat the oven to 200°C/400°F/Gas 6 and place a baking sheet in the oven to heat up.

2 Place the pastry ingredients into a food processor and whizz until they just bind together. Alternatively, sift the flour into a bowl, add the butter and rub in until the mixture resembles fine breadcrumbs. Stir in the icing sugar and then add the egg and mix until ingredients just bind together. Knead the pastry very lightly to form a ball, wrap it in cling film and leave to chill in the refrigerator while preparing the topping.

3 To make the topping, melt the butter in a saucepan and add the sugar and water. Stir over a gentle heat until the sugar dissolves. Increase the heat and cook, without stirring, until the mixture turns a light golden colour. Pour into the base of a buttered 23cm (9in) round cake tin with a solid base.

4 Sprinkle the cranberries over the caramel and pack the apple slices on top, overlapping them neatly to fill the base of the tin.

5 Roll out the pastry on a lightly floured surface to a circle just larger than the tin. Place over the top of the apples, tucking the edges down well. Place the tin on the hot baking sheet and bake in the centre of the oven for 30–40 minutes, or until the pastry is pale golden in colour.

6 Remove the tin from the oven and leave to settle for about 5 minutes. Then place a plate over the top and invert to turn out – use a plate with a rim and take care in case any of the hot caramel runs off the top. Serve immediately with cream.

Cook's tip
•**Choose firm, crisp, dessert apples for this recipe as they retain their shape better than cooking apples.**

Rich chocolate flan

The filling in this flan is very rich and creamy so only serve small slices!
The addition of some raspberries when serving adds a tart contrast to the flan.

15 minutes preparation time plus chilling
30 minutes cooking time
486 Kcal per portion
35.4g fat per portion of which
20.5g is saturated
8–10 servings
Suitable for vegetarians

For the pastry:
Plain flour 110g (4oz)
Cocoa powder 2 tbsp
Icing sugar 2 tbsp
Unsalted butter 75g (3oz), cubed
Egg yolk 1

For the filling:
Plain chocolate 200g (7oz)
Unsalted butter 150g (5oz)
Eggs 2
Egg yolks 3
Caster sugar 50g (2oz)
Cocoa to dust
Raspberries to serve

Cook's tip
•**Sift the cocoa powder over the top of the flan using a tea strainer rather than a sieve as you'll then have more control as to where the powder goes.**

1 Preheat the oven to 200°C/400°F/ Gas 6. Sift the flour, cocoa powder and icing sugar into a bowl. Rub in the butter until the mixture resembles fine breadcrumbs. Add the egg yolk and work into the mixture using a round-bladed knife.

2 Wrap the dough in cling film and chill for 10–15 minute. Butter a 23cm (9in) fluted flan tin and roll out the dough to line the tin. Prick the pastry base with a fork and chill the case for at least 10 minutes.

3 Place the flan tin on a baking sheet, cover the pastry with baking parchment and fill with baking beans. Bake in the centre of the oven for 12 minutes, then remove the paper and baking beans and continue cooking for a further 3–5 minutes, until the pastry is light golden in colour. Remove the case from the oven and reduce the temperature to 190°C/ 375°F/Gas 5.

4 To make the filling, melt together the chocolate and butter, in a microwave oven or in a bowl over a pan of hot water. Remove from the heat and beat in the eggs, egg yolks and caster sugar. Pour the chocolate mixture into the pastry case and bake in the centre of the oven for 10–12 minutes, until the filling has just set in the centre.

5 Remove the tin from the oven and leave to cool before removing the flan. Chill before serving so that it's easier to cut. Dust the top with cocoa powder and scatter over a few raspberries just before serving.

Hearty Hogmanay tart

Celebrate the New Year with a slice of this deliciously moreish tart. It's just wonderful with a generous dollop of crème fraîche.

15 minutes preparation time
25 minutes cooking time
262 Kcal per slice
14.7g fat per slice of which
6.5g is saturated
10 slices
Suitable for vegetarians

Shortcrust pastry 225g (8oz)

Marmalade 4 tbsp

Butter 50g (2oz), softened

Caster sugar 50g (2oz)

Egg 1, lightly beaten

Madeira cake crumbs 50g (2oz)

Ground cinnamon 1 tsp

Ground almonds 50g (2oz)

Raisins 110g (4oz)

Clementine 1, cut into slices which are then halved, for decoration

Crème fraîche to serve

Ground cinnamon for dusting

1 Preheat the oven to 200°C/400°F/ Gas 6. Roll out the pastry and place in a lightly greased 20cm (8in) flan tin. Spread the marmalade evenly over the pastry.

2 In a large bowl, cream the butter and sugar until light and fluffy. Add the egg, cake crumbs, cinnamon and ground almonds and mix well. Fold in the raisins and spoon the mixture into the pastry case.

3 Bake the tart in the oven for 20–25 minutes until the topping turns golden. Remove from the oven and decorate with the clementine slices. Serve warm with crème fraîche dusted with ground cinnamon.

Decorating with clementine slices adds colour and flavour. They also provide a sharp, citrusy contrast to the rich sweetness of the filling.

Cook's tip
•To help turn the pastry into its round shape, give it a quarter turn after each roll. As usual, make the round slightly larger than is actually needed to line the dish.

Mincemeat croissants

Try these croissants using ready-made croissant dough as an unusual alternative to pastry mince pies.

10 minutes preparation time
15 minutes cooking time
103 Kcal per croissant
5.6g fat per croissant of which
2.8g is saturated
12 croissants

Chilled croissant dough
240g carton
Mincemeat 4–6 tbsp
Flaked almonds 1–2 tbsp
Icing sugar for dusting

Cook's tip
•**Take care not to overfill the croissants or the mincemeat will bubble out during cooking.**

1 Preheat the oven to 200°C/400°F/ Gas 6. Unroll the croissant dough and cut the triangles in half to make smaller triangles. Place a small amount of mincemeat at the wider end of the long, narrow triangle. Roll up the triangle to encase the filling and curve the ends together to make a croissant shape. Sprinkle over the flaked almonds and press them into the dough slightly.

2 Bake the croissants at the top of the oven for 12–15 minutes or until they have risen and are pale golden in colour. Remove from the oven, place on a serving plate and dredge with icing sugar before serving.

3 These croissants are best eaten warm on the day that they are made. If they go cold, reheat them briefly before serving.

Tropical fruit cake

This is an exotic fruit cake that uses pineapple, apricots, papaya and mango rather than the more traditional currants, raisins and sultanas.

10 minutes preparation time
2¾–3¾ hours cooking time
435 Kcal per slices
16.6g fat per slice of which
8.8g is saturated
16 slices
Suitable for freezing
Suitable for vegetarians

Dried ready-to-eat pineapple 250g (9oz)

Dried ready-to-eat apricots 250g (9oz)

Dried ready-to-eat papaya 110g (4oz)

Dried ready-to-eat mango 110g (4oz)

Glacé cherries 110g (4oz)

Dried cranberries 110g (4oz)

Butter 250g (9oz), softened

Light muscovado sugar 250g (9oz)

Ground ginger 2 tsp

Eggs 4

Plain flour 275g (10oz)

Ground almonds 50g (2oz)

Rum 6 tbsp

Cook's tips
•**For storage, wrap the cake in baking parchment and foil and keep in a cool dry place for up to 3 months.**
•**For freezing, wrap the cake as for storing, and then you can freeze it for up to 6 months.**

1 Preheat the oven to 150°C/300°F/ Gas 2 and line a 20cm (8in) round cake tin with baking parchment.

2 Chop the pineapple, apricots, papaya, mango and cherries into small pieces and mix together with the dried cranberries.

3 In a large bowl, cream the butter and sugar together, until the mixture is light and fluffy and pale in colour. Beat in the ground ginger.

4 Gradually beat in the eggs one at a time along with a dessertspoon of flour with each egg. Fold in the remaining flour, ground almonds and the dried fruit mixture.

5 Spoon into the cake tin and use a damp hand to smooth the top.

6 Bake in the centre of the oven, for 2¾–3¾ hours, covering the cake with a sheet of baking parchment if it starts to brown too quickly. The cake is ready when a skewer comes out clean after being inserted into the cake. If any mixture is sticking to the skewer, then cook the cake for a little longer.

7 Remove the cake from the oven and leave it to cool in the tin to ensure the sides stay straight. After about 30 minutes, spoon the rum over the top of the warm cake and then leave the cake to cool completely.

Cinnamon stars

These biscuits are soft and chewy when baked. Wrap in pretty, festive paper and give to friends and relations who visit over Christmas.

15 minutes preparation time plus chilling
25 minutes cooking time
65 Kcal per biscuit
4g fat per biscuit of which
0.3g is saturated
35–40 biscuits
Suitable for vegetarians

Egg whites 2
Icing sugar 175g (6oz)
Ground cinnamon 2 tsp
Ground almonds 250g (9oz)
Lemon juice 2–3 tsp

1 Whisk the egg whites until stiff, fold in the icing sugar and cinnamon and whisk again until the mixture is of thick dropping consistency. Spoon about 6 tbsp of this meringue mixture into a small bowl, cover it and reserve. Continue whisking the rest of the mixture until it forms stiff peaks, then fold in the ground almonds and lemon juice and mix to a thick paste.

2 Form into a ball, wrap in cling film and chill in the fridge for about 1 hour, or until the mixture is firm enough to handle.

3 Preheat the oven to 200°C/400°F/ Gas 6 and butter 2–3 baking sheets. Roll the dough out between two sheets of baking parchment until it's about 5mm (¼in) thick.

4 Use a 2.5cm (1in) diameter star cutter to cut out shapes, then place on the baking sheets. Re-roll the trimmings and repeat the cutting out until all the paste is used up.

5 Bake the stars in the oven for 7–8 minutes, then remove from the oven. Reduce the oven temperature to 110°C/225°F/Gas ¼.

6 Use a pastry brush to paint the reserved meringue mixture over the top of the biscuits. Return the stars to the oven for about 15 minutes until the meringue has dried out but not browned. Remove the stars from the oven and transfer to a wire rack to cool. The biscuits will keep for up to 2 weeks if stored in a cool place in an airtight container.

These spicy biscuits make unusual decorations for place settings. Try different cutters to make alternative shapes to match the season or theme.

Cook's tip
•**Ensure that both the bowl and beaters are grease-free before making the meringue, otherwise the mixture will not whisk up to the full volume.**

Index